Contents

Data Protection Pocket Guide

Essential Facts at Your Fingertips

Second edition

Data Protection Pocket Guide

Essential Facts at Your Fingertips

Second edition

NFJ McKilligan
NHE Powell

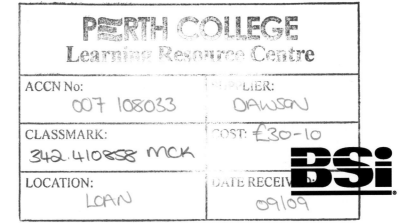

First published in the UK in 2009

by
BSI
389 Chiswick High Road
London W4 4AL

First edition published December 2004
Reprinted 2007

Typeset in Caslon Pro and Franklin Gothic by Monolith – http://www.monolith.uk.com
Printed in Great Britain by Berforts Group, www.berforts.co.uk

British Library Cataloguing in Publication Data
A catalogue record for this book is available from the British Library

ISBN 978-0-580-67561-4

Foreword

BSI would like to thank the Data Protection Editorial Board and the representatives of the following authoritative bodies for their assistance in reviewing this book.

- Barclays Bank plc
- Batchelor Associates
- Centrica plc
- Deloitte and Touche
- Department of Health
- Egg plc
- Essex Police
- Financial Services Authority (FSA)
- General Medical Council
- Information Commissioner's Office
- The London Boroughs Data Protection Group
- European Privacy Partnership

About the authors

Nicola McKilligan is a privacy and information law consultant with over 13 years experience of advising businesses on compliance with UK, European and global data privacy laws. She has worked as a Strategic Policy and International Officer for the UK Data Protection Commissioner (now Information Commissioner) and has been an in-house Data Privacy Officer for British Gas and Accenture. She is editor of the *World Data Protection Report* and is an experienced technical writer.

Naomi Powell is a risk adviser who holds professional qualifications in data protection, financial crime prevention and training practice. She began her data protection career at the Information Commissioner's Office, working in the Registration, Policy and Compliance teams. Her practical and common sense approach to compliance was developed as a data protection officer and privacy consultant in the financial services and energy sectors.

Preface to the Second Edition

This book is a guide to complying with the Data Protection Act 1998. It provides an overview of data protection law and practical advice and guidance for small organizations looking to comply with the spirit of the new British Standard for Data Protection: BS 10012. This second edition also contains new chapters on using CCTV systems in a way that complies with the law, maintaining ongoing compliance, updates on keeping data secure. The case studies are taken from the *Information Commissioner's Annual Reports* or press releases.

The Data Protection Act sets out rules that must be followed wherever personal information is processed for anything other than a domestic purpose. The Data Protection Act is the primary piece of legislation which governs compliance in this area but organizations can also choose to comply on a voluntary basis with the British Standard BS 10012: *Data protection — Specification for a personal information management system*, which provides additional requirements for data protection compliance.

How this book relates to BS 10012

This book complements BS 10012 but if you want to comply with the standard you will also need to refer to its requirements by referencing the full text of BS 10012 itself. This book does not recreate all the requirements of the standard in full but merely provides some guidance on its practical implementation.

If you are not intending to implement BS 10012 in full but would still like to adopt some of its practical requirements you can follow the advice in this book. This may be particularly useful if you are a very small business that would otherwise find it difficult to implement the whole of BS 10012.

Who should read this book?

This book is intended to be used by anyone who needs to understand their obligations under the law. In particular, it provides practical, simple and easy to follow advice for small businesses, charities, unincorporated members' clubs and anyone else who does not have the benefit of a large in-house compliance department. It is also a useful quick reference for managers and executives who are responsible for data protection compliance but who do not need an in-depth technical knowledge of the subject.

The Data Protection Act has a wide scope. Most organizations in the UK as well as individuals running their own businesses need to comply to some extent with its provisions.

If you or your organization operate in breach of the law when processing personal information you may incur civil, and sometimes criminal, liability. The adverse publicity may also cost you your business or ruin your organization's reputation.

You do not need to be doing very much with personal information to find yourself having to comply with the Data Protection Act.

Have a quick look at the list below. Do you:

- hold contact details for customers on computer?

- keep copies of invoices from suppliers?

- have an overflowing filing cabinet in the corner that contains personal information?

- telephone customers or other individuals to enlist support or business?

- publish images on the internet?

- have staff working alongside you?

- use third-party outsourcers to do work for you?

- have a CCTV system?

- use portable devices such as laptops, palmtops and mobile phones in your organization or business?

If any of the above applies to you, you will probably need to comply with the Data Protection Act.

Why you?

Information on individuals is a valuable asset and like your other assets needs to be properly protected. Apart from making good business sense, the reputation and success of your organization can be under threat if you do not make looking after personal information your priority. Without it, you would not be able to function as an organization. With it, you can create, maintain and build relationships of mutual benefit with your customers, clients, suppliers, supporters, investors and staff, who in turn will recommend you to their customers, clients, suppliers, supporters, investors and staff. A review of the *Information Commissioner's Annual Reports* shows that, so far, the majority of prosecutions under the law have been directed at small businesses that were either unaware of the law or failed to ensure compliance with it while running their business.

Why this book?

There are a number of detailed law books and guides available that will take you through the requirements of the Data Protection Act but most organizations or individuals need to understand the practical application of the law and how it applies to them. This book provides you with this basic practical advice to help make compliance with the Data Protection Act easier.

This book is also helpful because it includes additional information about compliance, drawn from BS 10012, which can help you make sure that your approach to data protection compliance is fully effective.

This book relates the requirements of the law directly to the way you process your customer, client or contact information. It also explains what you have to do and provides examples of how to do it. In addition, it provides specific guidance for businesses or other organizations operating in high risk areas.

What does this book cover?

This book covers all the requirements of the Data Protection Act, and by the end of it you will be able to:

- identify what personal information you can legally collect and use;

- know what you can and cannot do with the personal information you have collected;

- understand the law as it applies to your particular business or activity;

- deal with data protection 'emergencies' such as requests for access to information from individuals, bad publicity and investigation by the Information Commissioner;

- keep on the right side of the law and avoid compensation, hefty fines or imprisonment;

- benefit from improved data management and a better relationship with customers, clients and other contacts;

- monitor and review your processes and procedures for compliance in line with the requirements of BS 10012.

Because this book is a basic guide to the Data Protection Act, we do not cover related legal topics such as compliance with the Human Rights Act, freedom of information legislation or laws that cover the interception or regulation of communications in any detail. Other guidance is available from BSI that addresses these issues in more detail.

Structure of this book

The law applies to personal information from the moment of collection of that information to its destruction, and to all things that happen to that information in between – this is the way in which this book has been set out. It is structured to reflect the life cycle of the personal information used by your organization and to take you step-by-step through what you need to do.

This book provides guidance on:

- notifying the Information Commissioner of your processing (a legal requirement);

- collection of personal information;

- use of personal information, including some specific advice for specialist areas;

- security and disposal of personal information.

Troubleshooting tips are also included to help with common queries.

Terminology

This book avoids the use of legal terminology and the complicated definitions set out in the law. We have, however, tried to ensure that all the definitions we use are consistent with BS 10012. The main differences are that where the law refers to 'personal data', both this book and the British Standard refer to 'personal information', and rather than referring to organizations that comply with the law as 'data controllers' (as the statute does), this book refers to 'you' and 'your organization'.

Chapter 1 – Introduction

Who must comply with the Data Protection Act?

All individuals and organizations who 'process' personal information for their own business purposes must comply with the Data Protection Act 1998.

Types of organization that process personal information and therefore must comply with the Data Protection Act include:

- small, medium and large commercial organizations including limited companies, partnerships, limited partnerships and sole traders;
- charities, churches, political parties, and public and state schools;
- self-employed health professionals such as GPs, opticians and dentists;
- hospitals and NHS trusts;
- local authorities and other public sector organizations;
- unincorporated members' clubs and associations;
- anyone who employs staff.

What are the rules?

The Data Protection Act contains eight principles for good information handling. These are that personal information must be:

1. processed fairly and lawfully;
2. processed only for specified and compatible purposes;
3. kept accurate and up to date;
4. relevant and not excessive;
5. retained for no longer than necessary;

6. processed in accordance with the rights of the individual whose personal information is being processed;

7. kept secure;

8. adequately protected if it is to be transferred outside the European Economic Area (EEA).[1]

Guidance on how to comply with these principles is the main focus of this book. Further information about the EEA is given in Chapter 8, *Transferring personal information overseas.*

In addition to complying with these rules, organizations and individuals who must comply with the Data Protection Act may also have to notify the Information Commissioner of the details of how they process personal information. Chapter 2, *Notification* deals with this requirement.

The law also contains a number of criminal offences that relate to the misuse of personal information. These are covered in the relevant chapters.

What personal information is protected by the law?

Any information from which a living individual can be identified is protected under the Data Protection Act as long as that individual is the focus of the information in question.

A few examples of data that might be considered personal information, providing that it is possible to identify a living individual from the information in question and make them the focus of the information, include:

- name and address details;
- health information;
- information in emails;
- email addresses;
- CCTV footage featuring the individual's image;
- call recordings featuring the individual's voice;
- photos, either digital or on paper;
- NHS numbers;
- National Insurance numbers;

---

[1] The European Economic Area or EEA consists of the member states of the European Union plus Norway, Iceland and Liechtenstein.

- full postcodes;

- information in a personnel file.

Information processed by automated means, such as on computer, is always protected.

Information held in 'manual' or paper-based files will be covered by the law to a different extent depending on whether it is processed in the public or the private sector.

If the paper-based information is processed by a public sector organization, it is covered by the Data Protection Act.

If the same information is processed in the private sector, it will only be covered by the law when it is held in a very organized way (for example information that is held in a paper-based filing system, where it can easily be retrieved because it is organized so that someone who does not have any previous knowledge of the system could locate the information they require).

When is an organization 'processing' personal information?

You will only have to comply with the law if you are 'processing' personal information. The Data Protection Act defines what is meant by 'processing', and the definition is very wide.

'Processing' personal information means doing anything at all with the information, including collecting, using, storing and destroying it. Even just reading or accessing information can be 'processing' it.

Examples of processing:

- collecting information via an application form, over the telephone or via a website;

- publishing information;

- selling information;

- using information for administration;

- using information for marketing;

- intercepting information;

- recording information;

- data matching, data mining or profiling;

- archiving information;

- reading information from a screen;

- disclosing or passing information to another organization or individual;

- shredding information in a personal file or erasing information from electronic media;

- making information available on a website.

As the definition of processing is so wide, most organizations that use personal information will find it difficult to argue that they are not processing personal information.

Data processors

The only organizations that might escape being covered by the Data Protection Act are those that only process personal information on behalf of other individuals or organizations under their instructions. Such organizations or individuals are referred to as 'data processors' under the Data Protection Act.

These relationships must be governed by a contract that specifically sets out what can and cannot be done with the information being processed by the data processor. If you process personal information under an outsourcing contract like this, the organization that is instructing you will be responsible for complying with the law, not you.

Examples of types of organization that will often be data processors include:

- mailing houses;

- IT consultants that have access to clients' personal information when servicing IT systems;

- waste disposal companies that dispose of personal information on behalf of another organization;

- printers that print material, such as business cards, that contain personal information.

If you are processing your own personal information, for example in relation to your employees, you will have to comply with the requirements of the Data Protection Act with respect to this information. (See Chapter 10, *Employers and employee information.*)

However, in practical terms, whether or not you are processing information on your own behalf or on someone else's, it is unlikely to make much difference to the safeguards that you are required to put in place. The main difference is likely to be that when you process on behalf of another, you will have to comply with the restrictions in any contract rather than the obligations set out in the Data Protection Act. However, these requirements are likely to mirror each other, especially in relation to the security of the information.

REMEMBER

Even if you are not directly affected by the requirements of the Data Protection Act 1998, you will probably be obliged to comply with its requirements under contractual arrangements.

Who enforces the law?

The Data Protection Act is enforced by an independent regulator – the UK Information Commissioner. The Information Commissioner also provides advice and guidance to those trying to comply with the law and has a helpful enquiry service that will provide advice on a 'no names' basis. There is also a Scottish Information Commissioner who has responsibility for freedom of information regulation in Scotland. However, only the UK Information Commissioner enforces the Data Protection Act in the UK.

For contact details for the UK Information Commissioner's Office, see *Sources of information* at the back of this book.

The courts can also enforce the law. Criminal prosecutions are usually brought by the Crown Prosecution Service on behalf of the Information Commissioner.

Chapter 2 – Notification

Notifying the Information Commissioner

One of the requirements of data protection law is that organizations are clear and transparent about the personal information they hold and how they use it. With this in mind, one of the Information Commissioner's key responsibilities is to maintain a public register, available on the internet, of individuals and organizations that process personal information. The aim of this register is to reassure the public by making details of the processing of personal information available to them.

Unless they benefit from an exemption, organizations that are data controllers are required to 'notify' details of their processing to the Information Commissioner on an annual basis so that these details can be placed on the register.

The notification form

The notification process involves the completion of a 'notification form' that must be submitted to the Information Commissioner, ideally before you start processing any personal information.

There are two parts to the notification form.

Part 1 includes:

- the name and address of the organization;
- the company registration number at Companies House (if applicable);
- contact details for the company;
- a description of the processing being carried out, to include purposes, types of individual, types of information, types of disclosure and whether any information is sent outside the EEA.

Part 2 includes:

- a security statement;

- trading names;

- a statement of exempt processing (for example, if you are processing information on paper-based files, which are exempt from notification);

- voluntary notification (i.e. if you are exempt from notification because you are a not-for-profit organization, or are only processing for core business purposes, but you decide to notify anyway).

How to notify

Not all organizations have to notify. You should check whether or not you fit any of the exempt categories set out in Chapter 3, *Exemptions from notification*, but if you are obliged to notify you have a variety of options when it comes to completing your notification.

Ways to notify

There are three ways to notify:

1. on the internet (www.informationcommissioner.gov.uk) – there is a step-by-step process to follow, at the end of which you will be able to print off the forms ready to post;

2. by telephone – this is probably the easiest way, as you have the benefit of being able to ask any questions you may have;

3. filling in a request form – by completing a request form available on the website and then faxing it through or posting it.

Templates for notification forms

If you request a notification form via the telephone or via the request form, you will receive a pre-completed template notification form that outlines the typical processing activities of your type of organization, for example:

- schools;

- independent financial advisers (IFAs);

- charities.

If you use the internet to request a notification form, you will be able to select the correct template for your business yourself.

If you have been provided with a pre-completed template notification form, it is your responsibility to ensure that it accurately reflects your processing. It is intended to be an overview, and the headings used are quite general to reflect this fact. If it does not cover one of your processing purposes, it does not mean you are doing anything wrong but that you simply need to complete an extra form.

If you are a larger organization, you may wish to consult with colleagues who have responsibility for certain areas, e.g. customer services or personnel, to see whether they agree with the current notification entry.

Payment

The fee for notification is currently £35 per annum, which is VAT exempt. If you set up a direct debit, the renewal takes place automatically, therefore removing the risk that you miss the renewal date and are therefore processing illegally until you re-apply.

NB At the time of writing the fees for notification are currently under review and may be increased for some organizations. Please check with the Information Commissioner's Office for the latest position.

Organizations can notify the Information Commissioner directly. There are companies that offer a service to notify on your behalf. They target organizations that do not appear on the public register. They will forward your completed forms to the Information Commissioner and ask for an additional fee on top of the standard charge.

Such services are not usually cost effective. This section of the book takes you step-by-step through the notification process so that you can complete your notification yourself without incurring any further costs.

Where does your money go?

The revenue from the notification scheme is used to repay the 'grant-in-aid' that the Government supplies to fund the Information Commissioner's work.

If you stop processing personal information in a year when you have already paid for the notification, the fee will not be refunded.

What happens next?

After submitting your completed form by post, you will receive an acknowledgement letter from the Information Commissioner's Office. The forms will be subject to a preliminary check to ensure they are in order. If there is a problem, the Information Commissioner's Office will contact you, so ensure that the contact details given on the form are those for your office hours.

The notification takes effect from the day it is received at the Information Commissioner's Office, and in order to be certain that the forms are received by a certain date, they could be sent by recorded delivery.

When your notification has been entered onto the register, you will receive a copy of your register entry.

What are the consequences of failing to notify?

CRIMINAL LIABILITY

Failure to notify (unless exempt) and failure to keep a notification entry up to date is a 'strict liability' criminal offence, i.e. there is no defence to mitigate the charge. If you are caught out you will need to hold up your hands and accept the consequences. No excuses will be accepted.

What information is on the register and who has access to it?

Individuals can access the register to find out what types of personal information are being processed by an organization. They can use it to obtain contact details if they want to exercise their rights under the Data Protection Act, for example to opt out of marketing or to make a subject access request.

Each entry on this register contains details of the company and the purposes for which they process personal information. Each purpose heading contains further details on the individuals (for example customers, staff and suppliers), types of information held on these individuals, and any further disclosures or transfers of this information. The organization also has to give the Commissioner information about its security measures. However, for obvious reasons, these are not posted on the internet.

CRIMINAL LIABILITY

You do not have to display the register entry, but neither should you file it away too far from reach. You will need to keep it under review to ensure that it is accurate, as you are obliged to reflect any changes in your processing as soon as practicable and in any case within 28 calendar days, otherwise you are guilty of a criminal offence. For example, if you have indicated in your notification that you will only use personal information for administrative purposes but you now wish to use the information for marketing, you must update your notification to reflect this.

You will also be given a notification number. Some organizations choose to include this on their documentation, but an individual can search the public register just as easily using a company's postcode or company number.

Maintenance of a notification

Security is one of the biggest considerations under the Data Protection Act, and with this in mind, you will be issued with a security number that will need to be quoted in any contact regarding the register entry. By keeping this number confidential, you will guard against anyone, maliciously or otherwise, making changes to the notification that could ultimately lead to liability for a criminal offence.

Forms to add an additional purpose and to make any amendments to your register entry are available on the website or on request. There is no charge for making a change to a notification entry.

Changes of legal entity

Each legal entity has to have its own notification. If there is a change in legal entity, e.g. from sole trader to partnership, partnership to limited company or one company takes over another, a new notification entry will have to be submitted as entries are non-transferable.

Renewing the register entry

About one month prior to the expiry date you will receive renewal forms from the Information Commissioner's Office. If you have set up a direct debit, this renewal will take place automatically. If you miss the expiry date you will have to make a new notification application as it is not possible to renew an entry once it has expired.

Renewal time is a good prompt to check your register entry to ensure that it still reflects your processing.

Complying with BS 10012

If you are complying with the British Standard on data protection, you will need to ensure that you always maintain an up-to-date inventory of what personal information your organization processes and what it is used for. You may want to carry out regular reviews of this inventory to ensure it is up to date.

You can use your data inventory to collect and maintain the details of your processing in preparation for your annual notification. You should also set up a diary or other reminder system to make sure you are reminded when your notification is due for renewal. You should leave enough time between this reminder and the renewal date to let you review your current processing activities and make any necessary updates to your notification.

Notification agencies

There are a number of companies that send notification mailings to specific organizations that are not currently on the notification register, whether they are exempt or because they have failed to notify. They ask the organization to complete the standard notification forms, and then the notification agency forwards these to the Information Commissioner's Office for a fee, which includes the standard £35 notification fee. You are not obliged to respond to such mailings.

While many organizations offering these services are legitimate, some have been criticized by the Office of Fair Trading (OFT) for misleading organizations.

CASE STUDY

Data Protection Agency Services Limited, also trading as Data Collection Enforcement Agency, received an injunction under the Control of Misleading Advertisements Regulations 1988 following investigation by the Office of Fair Trading. The company has subsequently changed its name to Data Services (North West) Limited. This name change should mean less confusion as to the status of the company as one that offers a service, rather than an official government body.

It is important to remember that correspondence from the Information Commissioner's Office will always be on its headed paper and include its logo (comprising the initials 'IC' inside an oval). This can be cross-referenced with its website, or by calling its enquiry line.

Chapter 3 – Exemptions from notification

There are certain exemptions from the requirement to 'notify'. It is important to bear in mind that even if you are exempt from notification, you are not exempt from the requirement to comply with the Data Protection Act itself.

The relevant exemptions apply if:

- you do not process any information on computer;

- any processing you undertake is strictly on instructions from another organization, i.e. you are a data processor (see Chapter 1, *Introduction* for more information), or you only process information for personal, family or household affairs, e.g. a personal address list, Christmas card list or domestic closed-circuit television;

- you are a not-for-profit organization;

- you are only processing for the core business purposes.

Some of these exemptions are explained in more detail throughout the rest of this chapter.

Processing for core business purposes

If you are processing information for one or more certain purposes, known as 'core business purposes', you may be exempt from notification. These purposes are:

- staff administration;

- advertising, marketing and public relations;

- accounts and records.

Staff administration

You are exempt as long as your processing for this purpose is limited to:

- information on your staff, for example temporary staff, agents and volunteers;

- information that is necessary for employment purposes, for example qualifications, work experience, pay and performance, and health data;

- making disclosures with the consent of staff other than those that you are required to make as an employer, for example to the Inland Revenue, or to those organizations that have powers in law to demand it, for example the Child Support Agency.

Advertising, marketing and public relations

You are exempt as long as your processing for this purpose is limited to:

- information on individuals, for example customers, suppliers and supporters, that you use for the purpose of advertising, marketing and public relations in relation to your organization;
- information that is necessary for advertising, marketing and public relations, for example name, address and other contact details;
- holding information only for as long as necessary for these reasons and not after the relation between you and the customer or the supplier ends.

Note that if you obtain information from a third party, for example a list broker, a charity or a similar business, then you will not lose this exemption from notification.

Accounts and records

You are exempt as long as your processing is limited to the following purposes:

- keeping accounts relating to your business or other activity carried out by you;
- deciding whether or not to accept a person as a customer or supplier;
- keeping purchase, sales or transaction records to ensure that payments and deliveries are made by or to you;
- planning purposes;

AND your processing is limited to:

- information about people that it is necessary to process for these purposes, and any disclosures to third parties without the individual's consent are only made where necessary for these purposes, e.g. disclosures to an accountant or courier;

  AND

- you hold information only for as long as is necessary for these reasons and not after the relationship between you and the customer or the supplier ends.

Not-for-profit organizations

Small clubs, voluntary organizations, churches and some charities may benefit from this exemption if their processing is limited to:

- establishing and maintaining membership or support for a body or association not established or conducted for profit; and

- any further processing that does not fall outside the core business purposes described above.

Voluntary notification

Having gone through the process of determining whether you are exempt from notification, you may decide to notify anyway. Why would you do this?

The case for notification

Individuals are entitled to contact you at any time and ask for information about your processing. You have to respond to this request within 21 calendar days of receiving a written request as it is a criminal offence not to do so (unless you can show that you have exercised 'all due diligence' to comply. This would not include the request being misplaced in someone's in tray). If you have voluntarily 'notified' you are not obliged to respond to these requests, although it is advisable to let the individual know that you are on the register.

The case against notification

As mentioned previously, failure to keep a notification entry up to date is a criminal offence, to which there is no defence. You have to ensure that you have procedures in place to keep 'on top of' the accuracy of the notification entry.

Chapter 4 – Collecting personal information

This chapter covers the first data protection principle:

1. Personal information must be processed fairly and lawfully.

Collection

Now that you have notified the Information Commissioner, you can begin to collect personal information; however, you must ensure that it is collected in a compliant fashion.

Personal information is protected by data protection law from the moment it is first collected to the time when it is eventually destroyed, and at all the points in between.

Fair and lawful processing

If you want to collect and use personal information for anything other than domestic purposes you must collect this information both fairly and lawfully.

This means that you need to think about how you are going to comply with the law before you approach individuals with a view to collecting their information.

If personal information is not collected fairly or lawfully it means that you or your organization may ultimately be prevented, by the Information Commissioner or the courts, from using this information in ways that are essential to fulfilling your organization's basic needs, such as marketing, fraud prevention or the sharing of information with other parties.

It is therefore very important that you start out by following all the rules set out in the law that cover the obtaining of personal information.

There are three steps you must follow in order to ensure any collection of information is fair and lawful, and these three steps can be summarized by the following.

1. Ensure that you have a legitimate reason for needing to process the personal information (reasons are limited to those set out in the Data Protection Act) and if you wish to process sensitive categories of personal information make

sure you can justify this (again, this justification is limited to the grounds set out in the law).

2. Before you collect personal information, make sure that the individual whose personal information is being collected knows who you are and what the information is to be used for, including details of any third parties to whom the information may be passed or with whom it may be shared. You should do this by providing a 'privacy notice' to the individual.

3. Ensure the collection of the personal information and its subsequent use does not break any law or breach any contractual term or duty of confidentiality.

The rest of this section discusses what is involved in each of these three steps.

STEP 1: Establishing a reason for processing the personal information

Before collecting personal information, you or your organization must demonstrate that you have a legitimate reason for needing to collect and use the personal information in question.

The law lists a limited number of reasons why organizations might need to process personal information.

Legitimate reasons for processing personal information

Do you process personal information for any of the following reasons?

- You have a legitimate business need to process the personal information.

- You have the consent of the individual to use their information.

- You need to use the information in order to ensure the performance of a contract with the individual or because you want to enter into a contract with that individual, e.g. you may need access to a job applicant's educational history and proof of qualifications in order to offer them a contract of employment.

- You need to process the personal information in order to comply with a legal obligation you have been placed under.

- You need to process the information in order to save the individual's life or protect them from grave harm.

- You exercise a statutory function, administer justice or carry out some other function of a public nature that is in the public interest and requires the processing of the personal information.

If at least one of the above reasons applies to you then you will be able to begin processing personal information providing it is not classified as sensitive information (see *What is sensitive information?* below for more information).

In most cases it will be simple enough for an organization to establish a legitimate business interest in processing the personal information, i.e. that processing the information is necessary for the organization to function.

This will cover most uses that will be made of personal information, including marketing. However, you must always ensure that anything you intend to do with the information will not invade the privacy of the individual who has provided their information otherwise you may lose the right to rely on this ground.

A private investigator may want to sell information about a celebrity's spending habits using information that he has obtained from 'dumpster diving' (i.e. going through the celebrity's bins). While the private investigator might see a business benefit in such an activity, the invasion of the celebrity's privacy might outweigh the business need, and the investigator might need to find another ground for using the information or rely on an exemption from the Data Protection Act 1998.

If you cannot show a legitimate business need, you will need to satisfy one of the other grounds.

What is sensitive information?

Some personal information is subject to special protection under the Data Protection Act because it is regarded as being sensitive. Sensitive information includes information about an individual's:

- racial or ethnic origin;
- political opinions;
- religious beliefs (or other beliefs of a similar nature);
- trade union membership;
- physical or mental health or condition;
- sexual life;
- commission or alleged commission of any criminal offence by the individual;
- involvement in criminal proceedings in relation to any offence that has been committed or has been alleged to have been committed by the individual.

Where you or your organization want to collect the types of information set out above, you must demonstrate a particular need to use the sensitive information.

Grounds for processing sensitive information

Do any of the following apply to your processing of sensitive personal information?

- The individual explicitly consents to the collection and use of their sensitive information.

- The processing is necessary to comply with employment law.

- The processing is necessary to protect the individual or any other person from death or grave harm, and it is not possible or reasonable to obtain the individual's consent to the processing.

- You are a not-for-profit political, philosophical, religious or trade union organization that processes personal information about its own members relating to the purposes of the organization, and the information is not passed on to any other individuals or organizations. For example, a political party could keep a note of the fact that its members were voters but could not disclose this information without its members' consent.

- The information about the individual has already been made public by the individual.

- You are exercising a statutory function or administering justice.

- The processing is for medical purposes and you are either:
  - a health professional such as a GP, midwife, optician, nurse, dentist, physiotherapist, or
  - a person under a similar duty of confidentiality.

- The information is to be used for equal opportunities monitoring on the basis of ethnic origin or disability, and you also provide safeguards, such as allowing individuals the chance to 'opt out' of this.

- You are providing a confidential counselling or advice service.

The police and other limited organizations may also process sensitive personal information in order to prevent or detect an unlawful act or for the prevention or detection of crime or other unacceptable behaviour including the investigation of child abuse over the internet.

If you cannot demonstrate that you need to process sensitive personal information for one of the reasons set out above, you can obtain 'explicit consent' from the individual whose information you are collecting to use this information. Even if you think you can rely on one of the grounds set out above you may still need to check with the Information Commissioner that you can do so, as special conditions may apply.

In 2004, the supermodel Naomi Campbell successfully sued *The Mirror* newspaper for invasion of her privacy. *The Mirror* had published a picture of Naomi leaving a Narcotics Anonymous meeting. As part of her case Naomi argued that *The Mirror* was processing her sensitive information, in this case information about her mental and physical health, without her consent. The case went to the House of Lords and Ms Campbell was awarded damages from the newspaper.

'Explicit consent' as a basis for collecting sensitive information

As the grounds for processing sensitive information are much more limited, the easiest way to satisfy this aspect of STEP 1 is to ask for the individual's consent to process this information. Any organization or individual can collect and use sensitive personal information where they have obtained 'explicit consent' from the individual whose sensitive information is being processed, without worrying about justifying the processing under one of the other more limited grounds set out in the law.

The key word here is 'explicit'. In order to obtain 'explicit consent' the collector of the sensitive information must have made clear to the individual whose data is being collected exactly what sensitive information is being used and for which purpose. The individual giving consent must actively indicate their agreement to their sensitive information being used in this way. This agreement should preferably be recorded, for example by asking the individual to sign a statement indicating their explicit agreement.

However, it is still possible to collect such consent verbally, for example, over the telephone.

CASE STUDY

A charity collecting information about sight-related disability in order to send out Braille versions of information might provide the following explanation when collecting the disability information over the phone:

Caller: 'You've explained to us that you are registered blind.

I'm just going to make a note of that on our computer so that we can remember to send you all your information in Braille format.

Is that OK?'

Individual: 'Yes, of course.'

The caller makes a note on the individual's record that agreement to record sensitive information was obtained.

In 2004 the Information Commissioner found that a local authority was processing sensitive personal information relating to citizens who were 'hard of hearing' without the explicit consent of the individuals concerned. Instead the local authority obtained the information about their hearing difficulties directly from their medical records without their consent.

The local authority argued that it had implicit consent from the individuals concerned, but the Information Commissioner found that as the information was health information and therefore sensitive personal information, explicit consent should be obtained in order for the processing to be regarded as fair.

STEP 2: The privacy notice

The privacy notice

Once an individual or organization has decided that it can satisfy STEP 1 and establish a reason or grounds for its processing of personal information, it must also ensure that its collection of the personal information from the individual is 'transparent', i.e. it must be made clear to the individual how their information is to be used.

This step involves the issue of a 'privacy notice' to the individual providing their information. This is the most important requirement of the law in relation to the collection of personal information.

The purpose of a privacy notice is to explain to the individual:

- the identity of the organization collecting their information;

- how the personal information that is provided will be used;

- any other information that the individual should be told in order to ensure the processing of their information is fair, for example:

  - a description of any other organizations that the information may be shared with or disclosed to;

  - whether the information will be transferred outside the European Economic Area (the member states of the European Union plus Norway, Iceland and Liechtenstein);

  - the fact that the individual can object to the use of their information for marketing;

    – the fact that an individual can obtain a copy of their information (see Chapter 9, *Using information in line with individuals' rights*, for more information).

The Information Commissioner has also suggested in its *Privacy Notices Code of Practice* (available from its website) that you also explain:

- how long you or other organizations will be retaining their information; and

- whether the individual will suffer an adverse impact if they do not provide their information, for example if they will no longer be entitled to receive benefits.

Compulsory and voluntary information

If you are collecting some information that is compulsory and some information that is voluntary, you should also make this clear when you collect the information. The individual can then choose whether to provide the voluntary information.

Security

Some individuals or organizations also choose to explain the security in place for the individual's information and to provide details of who to contact with any data protection concerns. However, you should be careful not to supply too many details in case you put your own security at risk, and you should not give false assurances about the protection that is provided by these measures.

The following is an example of a straightforward privacy notice used by a small business collecting information over its website.

CASE STUDY

Barbara's Bed and Breakfast will use the information you give to us, for example your name and contact details, to confirm your booking and provide your accommodation. If you provide us with details of any disability or special dietary requirements we will only use these details, with your agreement, to make special arrangements for your stay. We will keep your information securely and will not share it with any other organizations unless required to do so by law.

If you provide your email address to us we would like to send you details of special breaks and offers. If you agree to us contacting you by email in this way please tick ❏

The privacy notice must be provided before any personal information is recorded or collected or the subsequent processing of the personal information may be in breach of the law.

In 2003, a health authority carried out a survey that collected health information linked to full postcodes. This resulted in a complaint being made to a national newspaper that the survey was not entirely confidential.

The health authority had not realized that postcodes could be considered personal information even though they would sometimes relate to the address of only one living individual. As a result it had not provided a clear and full explanation of how the information would be used when it collected information from participants in the survey.

The Information Commissioner became involved and the health authority accepted that a clearer and more transparent notice should have been provided to participants in the survey.

How should the notice be provided?

How you provide the privacy notice will depend on the media you are using to collect information. It can be provided:

- verbally, where information is collected face to face or by phone;
- in writing, where the information is collected on an application form; or
- electronically, where information is collected via a website or by text message.

Explain the non-obvious

The most important consideration is that your privacy notice should explain all the uses that you would want to make of the personal information. It should especially make clear any uses of the information that would not be immediately obvious to the individual whose data is being collected.

The suppliers of the Innovations catalogue lost their appeal against an enforcement notice served in 1992 that required them to provide a privacy notice 'up front' at the time of collecting personal information that was to be used for marketing purposes by the company and other organizations with whom the personal information was shared.

Innovations advertised through media such as newspapers, television and radio. Customers buying products from Innovations provided their names and addresses and payment details when placing an order. They received no notice explaining to them that their details would be used for marketing purposes when they provided their information, but the acknowledgement form that they received later did feature a notice explaining how their information would be used.

The Information Tribunal held that Innovations must provide a notice explaining any non-obvious use of the information, including the trading and sale of the information to third parties for marketing, before collecting the information, for example in any advertisement encouraging an order to be placed. The Tribunal also held that the notice should be 'clearly expressed in ordinary language and placed in a position of reasonable prominence in the advertisement'.

If you fail to explain a non-obvious use of personal information to an individual you will not be able to use that individual's information for the non-obvious purpose.

Size is important

Where any privacy notice is provided you must ensure that the notice is not hidden in the small print of the application form or in separate terms and conditions that may not be readily available to the individual at the time that their information is being collected.

The notice must be clearly delivered, for example above the signature box on the application form, or it may not be valid.

CASE STUDY

Linguaphone, the home-study language course providers, lost an Information Tribunal appeal in 1994. At the appeal the Tribunal examined the privacy notices used by Linguaphone and criticized the company for providing the wording in very small print, which failed to provide a sufficient explanation of how the personal information being collected was to be used.

Changing the purposes for which information is used

As mentioned earlier, it is important to make the uses of the information described in your privacy notice as comprehensive as possible. If you have told individuals, via your privacy notice, that their information will be used only for certain purposes and you later decide to extend the uses to be made of that information into areas that are substantially different, you will have to obtain the individuals' consent to new uses of their information.

CASE STUDY

In 1998, British Gas was prevented from using personal information collected from customers who had not received an adequate privacy notice for the marketing of anything other than gas or energy-related products. British Gas wanted to use its huge database (which dated back to its time as a monopoly public sector supplier) for wider marketing and tried to rely on a notice that was served to customers after the collection of their information. In some cases the notice was served many years after the first collection.

The notice explained that their information would be used for wider marketing purposes. British Gas argued that if customers did not contact it to object to the new marketing purposes it could interpret this as consent to market to them. The Tribunal found that consent could not be relied upon where British Gas received no response from its customers.

How much detail is needed

It might be tempting for a small organization to use a privacy notice that is drafted in such wide terms that it covers everything an organization would like to do with an individual's information. For example:

> *'Let's Do It All plc may use your information any way it needs to for the purposes of operating its business'.*

This sort of approach will not be compliant with data protection law. You must provide enough detail in the wording of your privacy notice to make it clear what the data is to be used for. However, try to avoid giving so much detail that the meaning of the notice is obscured.

Other wording that could form part of the privacy notice

You can also use your privacy notice to satisfy some of the other requirements of the law.

Collecting consent

You can use the privacy notice as a mechanism for collecting consent where this is required for the processing of the personal information.

Consent may need to be sought via a privacy notice where:

- no other reason can be relied upon as a legitimate basis for processing personal information (see STEP 1, page 16);

- no other reason can be relied upon as a legitimate basis for processing sensitive information (see STEP 1, page 16);

- sending information outside Europe in instances where there is no adequate protection for that information (see Chapter 8, *Transferring personal information overseas* for further details);

- information was collected for one purpose but you now wish to use that information for another purpose, but have not told the individual(s) concerned.

Where you need the individual's consent to process their information you need to ensure that their consent is valid.

In order to be valid, consent must be fully informed and freely given. Where you want to include a clause gaining consent for processing in the privacy notice you must ensure that you give a very detailed explanation of exactly what it is that the individual is consenting to.

You should usually try to obtain proof of consent such as a signature, and at the very least the individual must give some active indication of agreement. You cannot obtain consent by sending out a letter to an individual to ask for consent and assume that their failure to respond or to object indicates their agreement to consent.

You must be sure the individual concerned has both understood and agreed to the uses of the information for which you were seeking their consent.

REMEMBER

In most cases it will be sufficient to ensure that the individual is made aware of how their data is going to be used. You will only have to seek a firmer indication of consent in the particular instances where the law requires it.

Marketing options

If you wish to use any information you are collecting for marketing purposes you must explain this in the privacy notice. However, the law also contains a requirement that you must allow individuals the option of choosing not to receive marketing material (whether by mail, phone, email or any other method). (See Chapter 9, *Using information in line with individuals' rights* for more information.)

Most organizations choose to allow individuals the chance to object to having their information used for marketing at the point at which their information is collected. The most common way of doing this is via a marketing tick box. This enables you to ask the individual to either opt in or opt out of marketing by ticking a box.

CASE STUDY

Random Partners Dating Agency would like to use the information you have provided to send you details of special offers. Please tick the box if you do not want to receive these marketing mailings. ❏

CASE STUDY

Internet Wizards would like to keep you informed by email of the latest deals and bargains available on our website. Please tick the box if you would like to receive our regular offers and updates. ❏

Providing tick boxes is the best practice. The Information Commissioner endorses the use of tick boxes, and this method is also recommended by the Direct Marketing Association.

Drafting your own privacy notice

If you are a small business or organization you might be daunted by the prospect of producing a privacy notice, but it is really not that hard. The important thing is to explain all the uses you might make of the information.

As discussed earlier (see Chapter 2, *Notification*, for more information) you will already be carrying out regular reviews of the uses you make of personal information in order to keep your notification to the Information Commissioner up to date. This notification describes the ways in which you use personal information. Make sure that the notification you provide to individuals and the notification you send to the Information Commissioner match. Your notification to individuals can be based on your notification to the Information Commissioner. Whenever you add additional purposes for processing personal information to your notification you should also update your privacy notice.

You must also write the notice in a way that is easy for it to be understood by the individuals whose information is being collected. Road test your notice on friends and colleagues to see whether they understand it.

If you are collecting information from vulnerable people or children you may need to adapt the wording of your privacy notice to make it even clearer. Privacy notices aimed at children should be written using language that they can easily understand.

You can always search for inspiration by collecting application forms and examples of privacy notices from larger companies operating in your field. However, be careful not to copy them word for word. The notice you provide must reflect the uses of personal information that are specific to your organization.

If in doubt you can also seek advice free of charge from the Information Commissioner's Office (see *Sources of information* at the back of this book for details), or you could pay a lawyer or a consultant.

Collecting data for sales, marketing or promotional purposes and buying in contact lists

Collecting data indirectly

It is easy to see how you might provide a privacy notice when you collect information directly from the individual to whom it relates, but it is more difficult to imagine how you can provide such a notice where such information is provided by someone else.

In general, even though you did not collect the information directly you will still be expected to send your privacy notice to the individuals whose information you now hold. Ideally, you should do this before you start to make any further use of their information.

If you would rather not send out your privacy notice to such individuals because you believe this would be too difficult, you may not have to, if you can show that undertaking such an activity would involve disproportionate effort. You must document your reasons for relying on this argument.

When considering whether or not you could maintain a claim for 'disproportionate effort' you should take into account the number of customers, the cost of the contact as well as the way you intend to use their information when evaluating whether or not you can claim that contacting them would involve disproportionate effort.

There are no hard and fast rules but, generally, the more intrusive the use of the personal information, the more likely it is that it will not be acceptable for you to claim that providing a 'privacy notice' would involve disproportionate effort.

You should also take into account the means of communication. If you intend to use the information for email communication, such contact is so cheap and quick that you will be able to contact the individuals easily and cost effectively. In those circumstances, you may not be able to sustain an argument for disproportionate effort.

CASE STUDY

'Borrow-a-lot Ltd' buys names and contact addresses to be used for credit checking individuals before marketing them with financial product offers via mail.

Credit checking is too intrusive to justify an argument for disproportionate effort as a search is left on the individual's credit file, potentially affecting their credit status.

Assessment: a privacy notice must be sent out.

CASE STUDY

'Great Offers Ltd' purchases the commercial electoral roll as it wishes to send a mail shot to 100,000 addresses in various postcodes.

The cost of the mailing becomes prohibitively expensive if additional text is added to the mail shot literature. 'Great Offers Ltd' takes the precaution of screening against the mailing preference suppression list (see Chapter 9, *Using information in line with individuals' rights*), removing the names and addresses of individuals who have requested that they do not receive marketing mail shots. In this case, 'Great Offers Ltd' does not provide a privacy notice because an argument for disproportionate effort can be justified.

Another option, in cases where the third party providing information is close to the individual such as a family member or partner, is to ask them to confirm that they have the consent to give information on that individual and provide them with the privacy notice to pass on to the individual concerned.

Using an intermediary

If you hire someone to collect information on your behalf, such as a market research company, you must still take responsibility for ensuring it provides your privacy notice to any individual whose information is collected. If you have a contract with such an intermediary, make sure the contract ties it into providing your privacy notice.

Collecting information from friends, relatives and other contacts

If you need to collect information about an individual via friends, relatives, carers or other parties related to that individual, you should try to obtain confirmation that the party providing the information has the agreement of the individual to whom the information relates.

This is particularly important when collecting sensitive information, although it may still be possible to collect the information without consent where the collection is in that individual's vital interests. For instance, where the individual concerned is a vulnerable person whose life may be endangered, their information should be passed on.

Collecting information on behalf of another party

Where you are collecting personal information on behalf of another organization or individual you will usually need to provide their privacy notice, not your own. However, if the intention is that both you and the other organization will make use of the information, your privacy notice should make this clear.

Collecting information for trading or sharing

Information is a very valuable commodity and small businesses in particular will often want to make maximum use of their information by sharing it or trading it with others. If you wish to share or trade information you must explain this in your privacy notice. If possible, you should name the organizations that you intend to pass information to and describe the uses that they will make of the information.

Keeping a record

If you are seeking to comply with the British Standard on data protection you should also keep a record of the privacy notices that you provide for as long as you are processing the information you collected using them. Even if you are not intending to comply with the standard it is a good idea to keep a record of the notices you provide in case of any dispute.

STEP 3: Collecting information lawfully

Lawful collection

The final step in ensuring that information is collected fairly and lawfully is the 'lawfully' part. In addition to following the rules for fair collection you must not collect information in any way that is in breach of any law, including the Data Protection Act and other privacy laws.

Personal information will also be collected unlawfully if it is obtained in breach of any contractual term.

CASE STUDY

In 2003, a travel agent left his previous employer taking with him a database of customer details. The travel agent then set up a rival business of his own and used this personal information to market his ex-employer's customers. The incident was reported to the Information Commissioner who prosecuted the travel agent for 13 separate offences. The travel agent was fined £2,600 and ordered to pay £1,000 costs.

You will also be collecting and using personal information unlawfully if you fail to comply with other statutes or law.

Criminal offences related to the collection of personal information

CRIMINAL LIABILITY – OBTAINING INFORMATION BY DECEPTION

You should never try to mislead anyone into providing information about another individual by misrepresenting the reasons for which the information is being collected as this can be a criminal offence. You could end up with a hefty fine and a criminal record.

Businesses that operate in the debt tracing, collection and private investigation industries should be particularly careful to avoid this as the majority of prosecutions relate to activities undertaken by organizations and individuals involved in such activities.

Small businesses and individual employees account for almost all of the Information Commissioner's prosecutions for the obtaining of information by deception.

CASE STUDY

In one case, a tracing agent was found guilty of unlawfully obtaining and selling personal information following a joint investigation initiative between the Information Commissioner, the Department of Work and Pensions, and Revenue and Customs.

These two government departments are regularly targeted by debt tracers and private investigators who impersonate individuals who have legitimate reasons for gaining access to the personal information. This is often referred to as 'blagging' information.

As a result of his conviction the tracing agent in this case was fined and ordered to pay costs.

CRIMINAL LIABILITY – PROCURING INFORMATION ILLEGALLY

It is also an offence to procure personal information illegally by offering to pay or asking someone else to collect information for you in this unlawful way.

CASE STUDY

In December 2001, the directors of a credit control company were found guilty of the offence of attempting to procure information illegally from Revenue and Customs. The prosecution resulted in the directors being conditionally discharged for 2 years and ordered to pay costs of £1,000.

CRIMINAL LIABILITY – SELLING ILLEGALLY OBTAINED INFORMATION

If you have obtained or procured information by deception, as set out above, it will also be a criminal offence to sell such information.

Chapter 5 – Using personal information

This chapter covers the following data protection principles:

1. Personal information must be processed fairly and lawfully;

2. Personal information must be processed only for specified and compatible purposes.

Using personal information fairly

If you collect personal information in the correct manner, you will have made good progress in ensuring your compliance with the data protection law. However, there are still some other requirements that must be taken into consideration when using personal information.

Once you have collected personal information fairly and lawfully, you will still need to ensure that any subsequent use that you make of the information is in line with both the individual's expectations and the terms of your organization's notification to the Information Commissioner (otherwise you will end up processing personal information in breach of the law).

As already discussed, if you have provided a privacy notice to individuals, bear in mind that you will be restricted to using the personal information collected under that notice in line with its terms. If you later wish to use the personal information in a totally different way you will generally need to go back and obtain agreement or consent to do so from the individuals concerned.

You must also make sure that you continue to use information only in ways that reflect the purposes of processing that you have described to the Information Commissioner in your notification. If you fail to keep your notification up to date, you could be committing a criminal offence. There is no additional charge for updating or changing an existing notification.

So remember, if you need to process information make sure that, for your current privacy notice or notification, you:

- obtain the consent of the individuals first;

- update your official notification to the Information Commissioner.

Conducting a privacy impact assessment

As mentioned in Chapter 4, *Collecting personal information*, you will always need to balance the interests of your business or organization in using personal information against the individual's right to have their information kept private. Some activities or processing that involves personal information may be seen as more intrusive than others.

For instance, processing sensitive information about individuals or operating systems that place individuals under surveillance, for example via GPS or CCTV, could be seen as very invasive.

Collecting large amounts of information about individuals or sharing or selling information may also be difficult to justify. If you are planning an activity or processing that may pose privacy risks to individuals the Information Commissioner recommends that you carry out a 'privacy impact assessment' first to make sure the processing you are planning is lawful and fair and does not breach the Data Protection Act.

The Information Commissioner has published guidance on carrying out these assessments, which is available on its website, as well as a useful checklist to follow to ensure that your processing is compliant with the law and fair to individuals.

The Information Commissioner also recommends that you should carry out your privacy impact assessment as early as possible, before you install the new system or start collecting and using the data. This will help you to ensure that you do not implement a system or process that proves unlawful and that may prove impossible or expensive to make changes to at a later date.

Buying personal information

When you buy in personal information, for example for a marketing list, it is always best to confirm that the organization or person selling the information has already provided a suitable privacy notice to the individual or individuals whose data is being sold. You should ask to see a copy of the original notice which should make clear that information may be sold or passed to other organizations and must explain the uses that you will make of the information.

The same considerations will also apply if you are buying a customer database as part of taking over a business, as you will need to ensure that you are not subject to any onerous restrictions as to how the customer information may be used. For instance, if you wish to use the customer or contact information for marketing you would expect this to have been explained in the original privacy notice.

If you suspect information you are being offered has been obtained either unfairly or unlawfully you should not purchase or use the information. These days it is not uncommon for business deals to fall through because of problems relating to restrictions on the use of customer information caused by the failure of a business to comply with data protection law.

Electoral register

If you buy contact information that is based on the current electoral register, you can be more confident that such a notice has been provided as the electoral register is split into two parts – an edited register that contains contact details for individuals who do wish their information to be made available for commercial purposes, and a register that contains contact details for individuals who do not wish their information to be made available. Any information you buy in that is based on the 'commercial electoral register' will have been collected fairly.

NB Never accept a mailing list that purports to consist of the whole 'unedited' electoral roll, including the contact details of individuals who have opted out of the use of their information for commercial purposes. Only limited organizations are allowed to use this information, for example the credit reference agencies and the police. Anyone else offering this list for direct marketing will be committing a criminal offence.

Companies House register

If you are compiling contact or marketing lists from the Companies House register, you may still need to consider compliance with the Data Protection Act, even though you may only be interested in contacting businesses rather than individuals.

Where you compile contact or marketing lists that contain the names of directors or company secretaries, this information will be personal information and will be protected by the law. You must therefore treat this information like any other personal information.

Where you only collect company details, such as the company name and registered office address, you will be able to make much wider use of the information and will not generally have to treat the information as 'personal information'. The one exception to this is where you wish to market to companies via fax or telephone. In such cases special rules will apply.

Chapter 6 – Data quality

This chapter covers the third, fourth and fifth data protection principles:

3. Personal information must be adequate, relevant and not excessive;

4. Personal information must be accurate and up to date;

5. Personal information must be retained for no longer than necessary.

Ensuring the quality of personal information

Once you or your organization have collected personal information, the law makes you responsible for safeguarding the information and ensuring that it is fit for its purposes. This includes ensuring the accuracy, adequacy and relevance of the personal information you use.

Keeping personal information accurate, adequate and up to date

Obviously it makes good business sense to keep your customer, client or contact information up to date and accurate. The chances are that you already have some procedures in place to help you do this.

However, it is important to remember that the Data Protection Act places a legal obligation on the organization using the personal information to take 'reasonable steps' to ensure the accuracy of the information in its possession. What steps are reasonable may depend on the nature of the information you are processing. If inaccurate information could have a serious impact on the individual, such as wrong medical information or inaccurate information about a criminal record, then you will be expected to do more to ensure that the information is correct.

CASE STUDY

A case study in one of the *Information Commissioner's Annual Reports* told the story of an MP who complained to the regulator on behalf of his constituent. The constituent had complained to his MP that the Child

Support Agency had wrongly recorded him as the father of a child and were trying to force him to pay maintenance. During the Information Commissioner's investigations it emerged that an error in 1986 had allocated the constituent's National Insurance number to the man who was the real father of the child. The Information Commissioner held that there had been a breach of the fourth data protection principle.

The law also gives individuals the right to ask for a copy of any information held in relation to them (see Chapter 9, *Using information in line with individuals' rights* for more information), regardless of whether the information is out of date or contains embarrassing errors. Individuals can also seek compensation if they suffer damage or distress as the result of inaccurate or out-of-date information being used, and they have the right to have inaccurate information corrected.

What reasonable steps must I take to ensure the accuracy of my organization's information?

Unfortunately, the law does not specify exactly what steps an organization or individual must take to ensure that personal information is accurate. However, it is likely that you would be expected to carry out a regular review of data accuracy where personal information is held for years rather than weeks or months, and is still in use. As good practice, you should try to weed out out-of-date contact details, customer records and any other personal information that you no longer need. Where the information is held on computer you may want to use software from external sources to match the data to ensure accuracy. A popular option for checking address and postcode information is to use the Royal Mail's postcode check software. If possible, you could also periodically send personal information back out to the individual that it relates to, to allow them to check the information, e.g. when you next contact a customer, you could verify whether their address details are correct.

What if the individual or someone else has provided inaccurate information in the first place?

Where information has been collected directly from the individual, your responsibility is to record the information that is provided correctly, although it may still make sense to make external checks regarding address and postcode details.

If you have collected information from someone other than the individual whose personal information is to be used, try to confirm this information with the individual wherever possible, especially when collecting sensitive information.

What happens when the accuracy of a statement is in dispute?

If an individual claims that a statement or fact recorded about them is inaccurate, but you disagree, it may be preferable to add a notice of correction to the individual's records rather than changing facts or statements you believe to be true. However, the individual could still go to court to prove their case and could force the changes to be made should the ruling go against you.

CASE STUDY

In 2004, a man made an access request to the police national computer that holds the UK's criminal records and crime intelligence information.

The man discovered that the police had recorded that he had committed several crimes. Fingerprint evidence found that he was in fact innocent and that the offences were actually committed by a criminal who had stolen the man's identity.

The police agreed with the Information Commissioner that although they could not erase the criminal record, as it was their only way of keeping a reference to the crimes, they would add comments to the record describing the physical characteristics of the man whose identity had been stolen to make it clear that he was not the criminal.

It is a matter of opinion

Opinions as well as facts that relate to living individuals are covered by the Data Protection Act. If possible, you should record actual fact rather than opinions. If you must record opinions, make sure that they can be substantiated by the facts.

REMEMBER

Remember that individuals will have access to any opinions about them that you have recorded, and could sue if an inaccurate opinion has caused them damage or distress. (See Chapter 9, Using information in line with individuals' rights.)

It was correct at the time but it is now out of date

In some instances the information you hold will be a 'snapshot' of information that was correct at the time it was recorded, but is no longer correct. If you can demonstrate a need to retain this information then you will not need to update it because it is now inaccurate. It can be retained as a 'snapshot' of what was accurate at the time.

A doctor records a diagnosis of illness on a patient's records. After the results of further tests on the patient, the doctor revises the diagnosis, and both the old and new diagnosis form part of the patient's notes. One is an accurate representation of the current state of the patient's health. The other is retained as a snapshot of the doctor's opinion at an earlier date. Both diagnoses should be retained to reflect the history of the patient's progress.

Keep it relevant

You should collect only personal information that is relevant to the purposes of your business or organization. You should avoid the temptation to record information simply because it may be useful at a later date. The information should also relate only to the individual whose information is being processed unless there is a good reason to combine the information, such as where there is a financial association between two individuals.

An individual who was applying for a job as a foster carer and for a position on a nursing course applied for a criminal records check.

This showed that in the late 1990s she had 'associated' with local drug dealers. However, after an investigation by the Information Commissioner, it was found that the information related to her ex-husband and not to her. When the police discovered this they deleted the information from her file.

If you wish to collect additional information from individuals in circumstances where the information is not strictly relevant for your main business purpose, but could be useful for a secondary purpose such as marketing, you could consider making it clear that some information that is being collected is mandatory and that some is optional. If you do wish to do this, you should ensure that any privacy notice you provide also spells this out.

Do not collect excessive information

Even if you do need information for your business or organization's day-to-day use, think carefully about exactly how much information you need to collect. After all, you may have to justify it if an individual makes a complaint.

For example, as an employer you may be entitled to use CCTV in your office buildings to monitor the security of your premises and staff. But you are not entitled to use similar cameras in more private areas, such as staff rooms and toilets, to collect information about staff timekeeping.

You should also remember that if you are collecting a wide variety of information you will need to reflect this in your notification to the Information Commissioner, and this will be publicized when the information is published on the internet as part of your notification.

CASE STUDY

In 2002, *The Guardian* reported that the Countryside Alliance was holding information on the financial, sexual and religious habits of its opponents using information from sources including private detectives and the police.

The Guardian obtained this information from the Countryside Alliance's notification entry published on the Information Commissioner's website. It later emerged that the Countryside Alliance had played it safe by covering all types of information and all potential uses of information in its register entry. A spokesman for the Countryside Alliance confirmed that no sexual or financial data were held.

Keep information for no longer than necessary

The law also requires that you should keep personal information only for as long as you actually need it. However, it does not set out any specific time limits for keeping personal information. It is up to you to decide how long you need to retain the information.

CASE STUDY

In 2003, the Information Commissioner reported investigating a case where a police force disclosed information which was three years old about a complainant to his employer. This resulted in the complainant losing his job. The information consisted only of allegations that the police had not pursued. The complainant did not know that these allegations had remained on his file.

The Information Commissioner requested that the police delete the out-of-date information.

You must be able to demonstrate either a business or a legal requirement for retaining the information. It would also make sense to document this in a retention schedule for evidential purposes.

As long as you can demonstrate a business or legal need for holding onto the personal information then you may retain it. However, when keeping the information can no longer be justified, it must be securely disposed of.

You may be able to keep personal information for longer than normally required for business or legal purposes where the information is to be used only for historical, statistical or research purposes. However, if you are retaining information for any of these purposes you must ensure that it is not used for anything else, such as making decisions in relation to the individuals whose information is retained. If possible, information that is being used for historical, statistical or research purposes should be depersonalized or made anonymous.

Chapter 7 – Disclosing and sharing personal information

This chapter covers the seventh data protection principle:

7. Personal information must be kept secure.

Making disclosures of personal information

If you intend to disclose information to any other organization or individual, you must explain this to the individual via your privacy notice unless the disclosure is covered by an exemption under the Data Protection Act.

There are a limited number of circumstances where such exemptions will apply. The main exemptions apply where you are:

- disclosing information to a law enforcement agency for the purposes of crime prevention and detection;

- disclosing information to a government agency for the purposes of national security;

- disclosing information to Revenue and Customs or other similar public sector agencies for purposes related to the collection of taxes;

- passing personal information to any other person or organization that has a legal right to obtain the information, for example under a court order or a statutory power.

However, you should always take great care when making such disclosures, and it is sensible to put some procedures in place to ensure the disclosure is defensible.

Other information sharing

If you cannot rely on an exemption that covers making a disclosure of information then you can only disclose or share information where it has been explained that this will happen in your privacy notice.

Sometimes you may even be expected to use specially agreed wording to describe the disclosure or data sharing. For example, if you are passing personal information to a credit reference agency or shared fraud database, such as the Claims and Underwriting Exchange (CUE) run by the insurance industry, you will need to include wording in your privacy notice that has been agreed between the credit reference agency or CUE and the Information Commissioner.

Normally, where special wording must be used, this will be made clear in the contract that allows you to use the shared services. If you do not use the wording you may find yourself having to rectify any problems caused by the data sharing, and you may even have to pay compensation.

Special rules for statutory bodies

If you are a statutory body or a public sector organization that exercises statutory powers, you may find that you have additional problems if your statutory powers do not allow you to share or disclose information in the way you want.

If your powers are determined under a statute then you must process personal information within the parameters of these powers.

If you act outside these powers when processing personal information you risk acting *ultra vires* and your use of the personal information will be unlawful and in breach of the first principle of the Data Protection Act. This will be the case even if you have explained any additional uses of personal information to individuals via the privacy notice.

FAQs

I have received a request from an organization that wants access to the personal information that I process – What do I do?

The Data Protection Act does not prevent disclosures being made. It simply puts in place parameters within which they can be made. It is not the case that you will always have to have the consent of the individual concerned to make a disclosure. Where a public body has powers in law to demand it, for example, there are provisions in the Data Protection Act to allow you to disclose it.

It is advisable that you require any requests for information to be made in writing, as this will help you from an evidential point of view should you be challenged at a later stage, as well as enabling you to verify the identity of the requestor by cross-referencing signatures or checking headed paper.

If you are asked for information by a public body (for example Revenue and Customs, the Child Support Agency or a local authority) it is the public body's responsibility to prove to you that it has these powers by quoting its powers under the relevant law on the documentation. These have to be powers to demand information, rather than to ask for it. If in doubt, contact the Information Commissioner's Office for advice.

I've received a request from the police – What do I do?

The police have no powers under statute to demand information, and so will take one of two routes when they are seeking information:

- Court order – They will put a case to the court as to why information is necessary for their investigations, and the court will issue an order to present to the named relevant organization. This is an effective, if potentially time-consuming, process given the time-critical nature of the police's work.

- S29(3) – This is an exemption in the Data Protection Act for the organization itself; it does not give the police (or any organization) the power to demand information, although it is often presented as such. The exemption gives the organization receiving the request the discretion to decide whether to release the information without breaching the requirements of the principles where the processing (for example, disclosure) is necessary for the prevention and detection of crime, or the apprehension and prosecution of offenders.

Your organization has to decide whether the information is necessary – that is, the investigation cannot continue without it. By looking at the nature of the investigation, for example fraud, and the type of information being sought, for example details of purchases, you will have to decide whether it is appropriate to release the information. If in doubt, ask for a court order.

If the police are carrying out an investigation on your organization's behalf, for example after a burglary, you will be able to release information under this exemption without breaching the Data Protection Act.

I've received an information request from Revenue and Customs – What do I do?

Revenue and Customs, as a public body, has powers in law to demand information for the purposes of carrying out its statutory functions. This may be requested under the Taxes Management Act. Section 35(1) of the Data Protection Act allows you to disclose information when the law requires it. Check with the Information Commissioner's Office if you are unsure.

I've received an information request from my local authority – What do I do?

Where the local authority has powers to demand information in law, then you can comply without breaching the Data Protection Act. It is the local authority's responsibility to outline these powers to you. Ask for further clarification if you are unsure. You could also ask the Information Commissioner's Office if you are in doubt.

I've received an information request from the Child Support Agency – What do I do?

The Child Support Agency, part of the Child Maintenance and Enforcement Commission, is charged with ensuring that maintenance is collected and paid to parents with custodial responsibility for children.

In order to carry out its statutory functions, it has powers under the Child Maintenance and Other Payments Act 2008 to require information from and about non-resident parents and parents with care from the relevant parties, employers of relevant parties and local authorities.

I've received a court order – What do I do?

A court order is a legal demand for information. If you receive one, you have to comply with it. The Data Protection Act makes special provisions for court orders.

Some tips:

- check to see whether the order is signed and dated;

- if you have any concerns about its authenticity, telephone the court clerk for confirmation;

- provide only the information that has been requested, no more, no less.

Requests from third parties and private sector organizations

What if the request has been made on behalf of the individual?

A request may be made by an 'agent' on behalf of the individual. Examples of agents include:

- a solicitor, accountant or the Citizens' Advice Bureau;

- a partner or spouse – double check your files to ensure that there has not been any recent change of circumstances, to ascertain that they are genuinely acting on behalf of the individual and not in their own interests;

- an individual with power of attorney;

- Members of Parliament.

A general rule of thumb is to verify that they have the individual's authority to act on their behalf, by asking for a copy of the written consent and cross-referencing the signature or telephoning the individual to confirm. You could set up a procedure where, after an approach by a third party, you issue a letter directly to the individual confirming that you are authorizing their agent as per their instructions. They will soon be in contact if there is anything untoward.

Another point to consider is what the consent actually authorizes the agent to do. Is it limited to a certain time period, or to a certain transaction, or is it all encompassing? If you have any doubts as to whether the individual fully appreciates the nature of the information that may be disclosed to the third party in question, for example sensitive information, you could contact the individual to confirm.

Requests from solicitors

Solicitors may request information under section 35(2) of the Data Protection Act. This provision works in a similar way to section 29(3) (crime prevention and detection) in that you are not obliged to comply with it. You can choose to do so if you are satisfied that the disclosure is necessary in relation to legal proceedings, for the purposes of obtaining legal advice or for the purposes of establishing, exercising or defending legal rights. In a nutshell, if there are possible or existing legal proceedings about to take place that involve the individual about whom you have information and their solicitor has made a request for that information, or you need to take legal advice concerning your own relationship with an individual, you can rely on this section to make the disclosure. Remember that this is at your discretion.

Power of attorney

In England and Wales, this can take one of two forms:

1. general or ordinary: where someone authorizes someone else to act on their behalf for a short- to medium-term period (for example if the individual is going abroad) for some or all of their affairs, for example investments;

2. lasting: enables another person to take decisions on behalf of an individual and can continue when the individual loses mental capacity. There are two types: property and affairs, and personal welfare; unlike ordinary powers of attorney, these have to be registered with the Office of the Public Guardian to have legal standing. An individual can appoint more than one attorney.

Note that, in England and Wales, the Mental Capacity Act 2005 replaced enduring power of attorney with lasting power of attorney. New orders could not be created after 1 October 2007; existing ones are still effective, but cannot be altered. The Office of the Public Guardian maintains registers of enduring powers of attorney as well as lasting powers of attorney and these registers can be checked, for a fee.

In Northern Ireland, powers of attorney can be general or enduring; the latter are registered with the Office of Care and Protection.

In Scotland, continuing power of attorney for decisions such as property, finance and personal welfare can be granted under the Adults with Incapacity (Scotland) Act 2000. A register is maintained by the Office of the Public Guardian (Scotland).

Check that you are happy with the documentation that has been provided to you, and make checks if you are unsure.

Retailers, banks and insurance companies

The Data Protection Act allows a disclosure of information where it is necessary for crime prevention and detection and the apprehension or prosecution of offenders. Although this is often used by the police, it can potentially be used by any organization that investigates a crime, for example fraud or theft. Remember that you are not obliged to respond to a request, but if you understand from the third party that your information is crucial to its investigation, for example CCTV footage, you can disclose it.

Typetalk

Typetalk is basically a telephone 'relay' service: a hearing operator acts as an intermediary between the individual and the person with whom they wish to speak by communicating verbally and via text message written by and to the deaf individual.

The key thing to remember is that the conversation is no different from a direct conversation with an individual; you speak to the operator as you would to the individual, and so the usual rules concerning, for example the privacy notice and information security, still apply. Typetalk and the individual will have their own confidentiality arrangements.

Points to remember when making disclosures

Check that:

- the request for information is genuine and carries adequate authorization – make telephone calls if necessary;

- the request has been made by an organization that can benefit from any exemption being claimed;

- any exemption applies in the case in question;

- a record is made of the disclosure.

The following advice should always be followed:

- never give out information over the telephone;

- always ask for proof that the person requesting the information is who they say they are and that they represent the organization they claim to represent;

- ask the person requesting the information to provide a written explanation of which exemption they believe applies and details of any court order or legal powers, including a reference to the relevant clause in any statute;

- require that a senior employee of the organization making the request signs any statements requesting the information;

- check whether or not the individual whose information is disclosed can be informed that a disclosure has been made and if there is no requirement to withhold this information contact them to let them know;

- keep a record of the time and date of the disclosure, what information was handed over and to whom. Also keep a record of the justification or evidence considered when the disclosure was made and all paperwork.

And finally, if in doubt, do not hesitate to seek further advice from the Information Commissioner's enquiry line or a legal adviser. A genuine requestor will understand your need to get it right; the individual whose information you are disclosing may not be so understanding if you get it wrong.

Chapter 8 – Transferring personal information overseas

This chapter covers the eighth data protection principle:

8. Personal information must not be transferred outside the EEA without adequate protection.

The UK Data Protection Act implements the European Union Data Protection Directive 95/46/EC.

All countries within the European Economic Area (EEA) have implemented the Directive and therefore have similar laws that cover the way personal information can be processed.

Outside Europe, the laws covering the processing of personal information may not provide the same degree of protection. For this reason European data protection law places restrictions on the circumstances in which personal information can be sent outside the EEA.

Who is in the European Economic Area?

The following countries are currently in the European Union:

Austria, Belgium, Bulgaria, Cyprus, Czech Republic, Denmark, Estonia, Finland, France, Germany, Greece, Hungary, Ireland, Italy, Latvia, Lithuania, Luxembourg, Malta, Netherlands, Poland, Portugal, Romania, Slovakia, Slovenia, Spain, Sweden and the UK.

The EEA is made up of these countries, plus Norway, Iceland and Liechtenstein.

The Channel Islands and the Isle of Man are not inside the EEA.

Personal information can only be sent outside the EEA where the organization sending it can guarantee 'adequate protection' for the information.

What is meant by 'adequate protection'?

If you want to send or take personal information outside the EEA, even where this transfer occurs within your own organization, you must assess whether or not it will be adequately protected.

In making this assessment, you must consider all relevant circumstances including whether:

- the country to which you wish to send or take the personal information has laws in place that will protect the information;
- you can protect the information by technical means such as encryption;
- you can protect the information under the terms of a contract.

(See Chapter 13, *Security and disposal of personal information* for more information.)

Safe countries

The European Commission has judged that a number of countries have laws that are similar to those in place in the EEA. These include:

- Argentina;
- Canada;
- Guernsey and Jersey;
- Isle of Man;
- Switzerland.

You can transfer personal information to these countries freely.

You can also transfer information safely to organizations in the USA that subscribe to the 'Safe Harbor' agreement, which is a voluntary compliance regime regulated by the Federal Trade Commission. Financial organizations are excluded from entering into this agreement.

You can check whether or not the organization that you are transferring information to subscribes to the 'Safe Harbor' agreement at the FTC website.

Technical measures

If the personal information is being transferred abroad by a method that essentially means that it remains under your control, e.g. you or an employee are taking the information on a laptop for a business trip, you could use technical means to protect the information, for instance by encrypting the hard drive.

However, you should still check whether or not the technical measures you are intending to use are lawful in the country to which the personal information is being taken. Customs officials can sometimes demand access to protected data held on laptops or other media brought into their countries.

Recording the reason for believing protection to be adequate

You should always document the basis for your decision, regardless of your reasons for believing there to be adequate protection for the personal information which is being transferred outside the EEA. This will help you evidentially should a complaint be made to the Information Commissioner.

For further information, see Chapter 16, *Contact with the Information Commissioner*.

What if no assessment has been made?

If making the assessments set out above seems too complicated, it might be useful to know that there are some instances where such an assessment need not be made.

No assessment need be made, for example, where:

- the individuals whose information is being transferred outside the EEA consent to the transfer;

- an approved 'model contract' or 'Binding Corporate Rules' policy is used to protect the information;

- there is a contract in place between the individual and your organization and it is absolutely necessary to transfer the personal information outside the EEA in order to fulfil the contract;

- the transfer is necessary in connection with legal proceedings;

- the transfer is necessary to protect the life of the individual;

- the transfer is part of personal information on a public register (subject to any restrictions on the use of that information).

Obtaining consent

REMEMBER

If you want to rely on consent for transferring the personal information outside Europe you must explain the transfer clearly to the individuals concerned so that they know exactly what they are agreeing to.

You should state explicitly what type of personal information will be sent outside Europe, what it will be used for and which countries it will be sent to.

If you know that you will be transferring the personal information outside the EEA, then, when you collect the information, you should include wording in your privacy notice to explain this.

Model contracts

If the transfer of personal information is to be made to another organization, such as a data processor in a country that is not within the EEA or on the list of 'safe countries', you can use a contract to protect the information.

The contract must be put in place between your organization and the organization to which you are transferring the personal information.

The safest option is to use a model contract as drafted by the European Commission. These contracts have been specifically designed to cover all aspects of the transfer. If you plan to use these, you must use them as drafted, otherwise they may no longer be sufficient for the transfer.

There are two versions of the model contracts:

1. a data processor contract – where the organization you are passing the personal information to is processing information on your instructions only for your business purposes;

2. a data controller contract – where the organization you are passing information to will be using the information for its own purposes.

The model contracts are available free of charge from the Information Commissioner's and the European Commission's websites.

Binding corporate rules

Large multinational organizations often face difficulties when they want to share personal information related to their customers or employees within their global group of companies. Where the personal information relates to European customers or employees it may be difficult to transfer this data to countries that do not offer adequate protection through their local data protection or privacy laws.

In such cases organizations can choose to implement a binding global data protection policy or 'Binding Corporate Rules' (BCR) throughout their global organization. This is then sent for approval to the data protection authority in the EU country or countries from which the personal information is to be transferred. In the UK, for instance, the Information Commissioner would need to approve the BCR.

The BCR must be backed up by appropriate procedures for ensuring compliance and also be made contractually binding on different parts of the organization and its staff.

Preparing and obtaining approvals for BCR can be very costly and time-consuming and is therefore often not an option for small and medium businesses.

Guidance on BCR is available from the Information Commissioner's and European Commission's websites.

Chapter 9 – Using information in line with individuals' rights

This chapter covers the sixth data protection principle:

6. Personal information must be processed in accordance with the individual's rights in relation to their information.

The law and individuals' rights

The Data Protection Act provides individuals with a number of rights in relation to the processing of their personal information. It is a requirement of the law that individuals and organizations comply with these rights when processing personal information.

There are six rights provided for individuals under the Data Protection Act. These are:

1. the right to obtain a copy of the information about them, plus a description of the type of information being processed, the uses that are being made of the information and those persons to whom their personal information has been disclosed;

2. the right to prevent processing of their information where the processing would cause them damage or distress;

3. the right to prevent the use of their information for direct marketing;

4. the right to be told about and to object to certain kinds of automated decision-taking;

5. the right to claim compensation where they have suffered damage or damage and distress as a result of a breach of the Data Protection Act;

6. the right to have inaccurate information about them corrected.

If you or your organization processes personal information, you must ensure that you are prepared to assist and allow individuals to exercise these rights in relation to their personal information. It is important to note that there are different timescales for complying with the different rights, and you must allow time for postage.

Further details of how to use personal information without infringing these rights is provided below.

The right of access

Allowing an individual access to their personal information

Any information that you or your organization is processing in relation to a living individual who is the focus of that information must be accessible to that individual.

This includes all opinions and facts that are recorded on any automated system, as well as some information held in paper-based files where this is set out in such a way that it is easily accessible.

Some information is exempt from this right; see *FAQs* on page 60 for further details.

What sorts of access requests are valid?

In order to be a valid access request the request must be made in writing. This includes requests made via email. The request does not have to mention the Data Protection Act 1998. You do not have to action a request made over the telephone, although it is good practice to explain your procedures if such a request is made, and therefore it is important that staff are aware of these procedures.

What exactly is the individual entitled to?

The individual making the access request is entitled to an exact copy of all the information that relates to them.

This could include:

- printouts of information from databases;
- copies of call recordings (where the call was recorded using an automated system);
- copies of emails;
- copies of CCTV tapes (where recorded using an automated CCTV system and where the CCTV camera was deliberately focused on the individual);
- paper-based information (public sector);
- information in a paper-based filing system where the information about the individual can be easily retrieved because it is so organized that even someone without a previous knowledge of the system could locate the information (private sector).

You also have to describe to the individual (in summary form) what types of information you hold about them, what you use that information for and whether or not you have disclosed the information to any other organizations or individuals.

You can either name or just describe the persons to whom any disclosures were made; this may depend on the numbers involved, and also on whether or not the individual has particular concerns about this particular aspect.

You must also respond to the individual even if you have no information about them, in order to let them know that.

You must also provide the copies of the information in an intelligible form. This means that the information must be readable (or watchable/audible) and any jargon or computer codes must be accompanied by an explanation of what they mean, e.g. if you add the code 'TC' to the files of troublesome customers, you must provide the code and an explanation of what it stands for to the individual as part of your response to their access request.

How long do I have to comply with the request?

You have 40 calendar days to respond to the access request (see Figure 1). The clock starts ticking once you have received all of the following from the individual:

- the written request;
- sufficient information to identify the individual and the information being requested;
- the £10 fee.

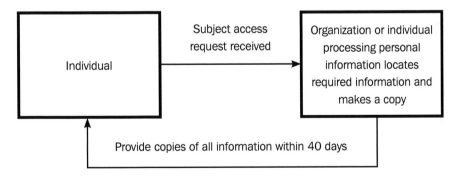

Figure 1 — Personal information and the subject access request cycle

Can I charge for the information and how much can I charge?

You can normally charge a fee of up to £10 for the information, but you can charge more in relation to some health records.

See Chapter 14, *Sector-specific guidance for using personal information.*

The right to object to direct marketing

Using personal information for direct marketing

Individuals have the right to decide whether or not they wish their information to be used for direct marketing purposes. If any individual objects to this use, you must respect it.

The wide definition of direct marketing

The definition of direct marketing covers many activities. It is defined by the Information Commissioner not only to cover those activities that relate to offers for the sale of goods or services, but also to cover the promotion of an organization's aims or ideals. This means that any promotional material sent out by any type of organization will be caught including:

- charities' campaign information;

- political parties promoting their cause;

- small businesses targeting their customers with news about special offers.

It also covers direct marketing via any media including mail, telephone, email, SMS (short message service, or 'text message'), MMS (multimedia message service, or 'video message') and fax.

The marketing must be targeted towards a particular individual. Marketing activities such as the distribution of leaflets in the high street or mailing addressed to 'the Occupier' are not covered.

Do I need to tell people that they can object?

As part of your privacy notice you must always explain to individuals if you are going to be using their information for marketing purposes. You should also ask them to either indicate their agreement to this or let you know if they object.

Where information is being collected via an application form or over the internet this is usually done via a marketing tick box. Over the phone you can simply ask the customer or client for their preference although you will obviously need to keep a note of this so that you can ensure that no marketing to that individual occurs.

Special rules for different marketing channels

While the Data Protection Act sets out one rule for direct marketing, the Privacy and Electronic Communications Regulations 2004 also introduce separate and additional rules for marketing via types of medium that are considered specifically intrusive.

These include direct marketing by:

- telephone and mobile phone;

- fax;

- email.

Marketing preference services

Individuals who object to receiving unsolicited direct marketing can register their details on registers managed by the Direct Marketing Association.

There are several marketing preference registers, but use of only the Telephone Preference Service (TPS – for individual subscribers), Corporate TPS (for corporate subscribers) and Fax Preference Service (FPS) is required by law. Further information is given below.

However, it is good practice to use other preference services to screen your marketing activity. The other preference services include:

- the Mailing Preference Service (MPS) for direct mail;

- the Email Preference Service (EPS) for email marketing;

- the Baby MPS for mail marketing to new mothers.

Details of all the preference services can be found on the Direct Marketing Association's website, http://www.dma.org.uk.

Telephone marketing

Being interrupted in the middle of your favourite TV programme by a salesperson can be annoying, so it should come as no surprise to find that telemarketing is on the list of intrusive marketing activities.

Where you are collecting information directly from individuals for telemarketing, you should always explain to them that you intend to use the information to make telemarketing calls and give them the chance to object.

In addition, if you wish to telephone individuals you do not know as part of a cold-calling exercise you are now obliged to screen the telephone contact numbers against a list maintained by the TPS.

This list contains the numbers of individuals who do not want to receive marketing calls. If an individual's number is on this list you may not call them unless you have separately obtained their consent to contact them for marketing purposes.

The rules extend to protect businesses, including limited companies that do not want to receive marketing calls. You now need to screen cold calls to businesses against a Corporate TPS.

CASE STUDY

In 2007 the Information Commissioner issued an enforcement notice against Weatherseal Holdings Limited after receiving numerous complaints from individuals who had received marketing calls. Some individuals had told Weatherseal that they did not want to be contacted for marketing whereas others had registered their number with the TPS. Individuals also complained that the callers from Weatherseal failed or refused to identify the company when making the call and would not provide a valid address or telephone number for contacting the company.

Marketing by fax

Marketing by fax is also considered to be particularly intrusive, especially in relation to direct marketing to individuals. This is partly because faxes cost money to receive and also because marketing faxes tend to be sent at night to save money. This is very annoying to the recipient if their fax machine is in their bedroom.

As a result, you need to obtain individuals' agreement to marketing by fax rather than just telling them that you will market in this way and waiting for them to object.

You will also need to screen any 'cold' faxes to businesses against numbers held by the FPS before marketing to them by this channel.

Marketing by email, SMS and MMS

Special rules also apply to marketing by email, SMS and MMS. These rules are set out in Chapter 11, *E-commerce*.

Processing that may cause damage or distress to an individual

Objecting to processing

If an individual is caused or believes that they will be caused either substantial, unwarranted damage or substantial, unwarranted distress, or both of these, as a result of your processing of their information, they can serve you with a written notice to stop the processing.

You have 21 calendar days to respond to this notice or you will be in breach of the Data Protection Act. In your response you must state whether or not you intend to comply with the request and to what extent. You must also let them know if you intend to continue with the processing despite the notice.

You must make your response in writing.

Individuals are not entitled to serve a notice if:

- they have already consented to the processing;

- it is necessary for the performance of a contract with the individual entered into at their request;

- the processing is being carried out to comply with a legal obligation or the processing is necessary to protect their vital interests in a life or death situation.

Claims for compensation

Individuals can also claim compensation in the courts for any damage and possibly distress they have suffered as a result of any processing that is in breach of the Data Protection Act 1998.

To claim damage they must show that they have suffered financial loss or physical harm as the result of a breach.

They are not able to claim solely for distress without having suffered additional damage unless the organization is processing their information for journalistic, artistic or literary purposes.

Don't let matters reach this point. Remember that the individual will only be entitled to compensation if you have breached the law.

If compensation is awarded it will reflect the loss suffered as well as any distress. There is therefore no limit on the amount you may be asked to pay.

Rights in relation to automated decision-taking

Fully automated decisions

It is possible these days to make important decisions about individuals based on a solely automated basis with no human intervention at all. In essence a computer rather than a person makes the decision.

This sometimes happens where CVs are scanned electronically to select job applicants for an interview, or where a person applies for credit over the internet and is refused based on criteria that have been applied by the computer.

Where such decisions have a significant effect on the individual concerned, as in the two examples above, then the individual has certain rights in relation to the decision-taking process.

An individual can write to an organization at any time and require it not to take any decision on this basis.

An organization that has already taken an automated decision also has an obligation to inform the individual concerned that the decision was taken on that basis.

The individual then has 21 calendar days to serve a notice on the organization employing the automated decision-taking asking it to reconsider the decision on a non-automated basis. The organization must respond to the request within 21 calendar days.

Some types of decision-taking are exempt from these requirements, including where:

- the decision is taken for the purposes of considering whether to enter into, entering into, or performing a contract with the individual; or

- the decision is required under statute, and there is a process in place for the individual to request a review of that decision by a real person.

Challenges to accuracy through the courts

You are already aware that it is a requirement of data protection law that personal information is kept accurate and up to date. However, should you fail to correct inaccuracies in personal data, individuals also have the right to go to court to obtain an order to force you to rectify, block, erase or destroy the inaccurate information. Where the inaccuracies have been disclosed to third parties the courts can also require you to notify these other organizations of the rectification, erasure, blocking or destruction of the inaccurate personal information.

FAQs – Responding to individuals exercising their rights under the Data Protection Act 1998

Dealing with subject access requests

I have received a request quoting section 7 of the Data Protection Act 1998 and asking for a copy of information held – What do I do?

Individuals have the right to ask for a copy of personal information held about them. This is known as 'subject access', i.e. an access request by the subject of the personal information. Remember that the individual has to be the subject of the information, rather than just being mentioned in passing, for example if they are copied into an email or are an attendee on meeting minutes. Where the individual is not the subject of the discussion this would not be considered to be personal information about that individual. This information may be held on computer, paper-based files or even media such as CCTV or audiotape.

Frequently these requests are made as the consequence of a complaint against the organization about alleged inaccuracy, or an unauthorized disclosure. However, they may sometimes be in relation to the individual's personal circumstances: a relationship breakdown, or simply putting their paperwork in order.

These requests can be time-consuming, and the maximum statutory fee of £10 may not cover your administrative costs. If an individual is requesting a particular piece of information, for example a copy of a letter, it may be easier and more cost effective to treat this informally rather than to go down the formal route of producing the entire file within a statutory deadline of 40 calendar days. Depending on the status of the current relationship with the individual, you may wish to clarify with them whether they are looking for something in particular, for example relating to certain dates or to a certain transaction.

Even if you are not processing any information on the individual who has made the request, and the information is not being processed on your behalf, you are still obliged to reply and let them know that this is the case.

Has the individual made the request in writing?

The Data Protection Act requires that the request is made in writing, which includes email or fax. If the request has been made over the telephone, ask for it to be confirmed in writing, or better, issue a form drafted for this purpose. This form should include enough information to help you to locate the information, for example relevant dates, nature of the relationship and account number. Ensure that the request is date-stamped on receipt.

Am I satisfied that the requests are being made by the individuals themselves?

A written request has the advantage of making it easier to verify the individual's identity. You should check that the signature (if available) and the address to which the information is to be sent match your files. Telephone the customer if necessary; you can check their requirements at the same time.

If the information in question is likely to cause distress in the wrong hands, for example, it is sensitive as defined in the Data Protection Act or may be commercially sensitive, you may wish to ask for additional proof. Examples could include:

- a copy of a document that is likely to only be in their possession, for example a driving licence;

- asking a question, the answer to which is likely to be known only by them, for example, the date of their last visit or their last purchase;

- asking them, if feasible, to collect the information and provide proof of identity when they collect the information.

If the individual has specifically requested copies of CCTV tapes, it is advisable to ask for a photo in order to help locate the images.

What if the request has been made on behalf of the individual?

See Chapter 7, *Disclosing and sharing personal information,* for further information.

Can I charge a fee?

The Data Protection Act allows you to charge a fee of up to £10. You do not have to charge this fee, and it may be worth considering waiving this as a goodwill gesture in certain circumstances.

There are different provisions in relation to paper-based medical records. See Chapter 14, *Sector-specific guidance for using personal information,* under *Health professionals* for further information.

What are the timescales?

You should comply with the request as soon as practicable – but in any event, in no more than 40 calendar days (as opposed to working days) after you have received the request in writing, you have received the fee (if you are going to charge it) and you have enough information to identify the individual and find the information they are looking for. You may wish to start collating information before you have all these items in place if you have concerns about your ability to comply within the 40-day deadline. However, it is worth bearing in mind that you may never receive the written request, especially if the issues behind the request have been resolved in the meantime.

If you do find yourself in the position where you cannot comply with the deadline, the best steps are to make the individual aware of that fact and to send them what you can, making them aware that there is further information to follow. As you are breaching the requirements of the Data Protection Act, there may be further action as a result.

Retrieving the information

You have all the information you need from the individual. Now you have to find their information. Remember to include the following information in your search:

- information processed by your organization across different sites;
- information processed by personnel working from home;
- information held in archives;
- data on computer records, including microfiche and emails;
- information on paper-based files;
- information recorded digitally or on tape (call recordings and CCTV images where appropriate);
- any 'back-up' information.

Permanent form

You are required to provide a copy of information in a permanent form, i.e. on paper or cassette unless this would prove impractical in terms of time and cost. In those cases you will have to provide an alternative, for example for the individual to visit your premises and view the information on screen.

Can I change the information?

The short answer is no. The request effectively triggers a snapshot of the information that is being processed on the date on which it is received. However, if you would normally have updated or deleted information had you not received the request, for example payments on an account, you can continue to do so between the date of the request and the date of the reply. This may have the effect that the information disclosed to the individual is different from that which was held at the date of the request; it may even have been deleted. The key point to remember is that you cannot deliberately alter it to hide something.

It is often at this point that you realize the value of having organizational guidelines for recording of information. Calling people names will effectively mean shooting yourself in the foot as far as that relationship is concerned. Keep information factual; your version of what constitutes angry and aggressive behaviour may be different from your colleagues' version, and their future transactions with the individual will be based on your comments. Stick to actual quotes, for example:

> the customer said he 'was angry because the order didn't arrive and would certainly do no further business with [us]'.

What additional information must be sent to the individual?

In addition to the personal information, you have to provide the context in which that information is used, for example:

- a description of the personal data (what type of information is held);
- the purposes for which it is being processed (why is it held);
- the source of that information (if available) and the recipients.

You can address these points in your covering letter or provide a hard copy of your notification (if applicable). Remember that sources of information are not covered by this and will therefore have to be specified separately.

The individual has asked for information under section 7(1)(d) – What does this mean?

Under this section, individuals have the right to be told the logic behind any automated decisions taken about them. This would not have to be provided in so much detail that you, for example, expose yourself to individuals who are trying to manipulate their answers or actions in order to 'beat the system'.

For instance, an example of a response in relation to a request that covered creditworthiness could be:

'We ask you to answer a series of questions about your personal circumstances and financial history. In addition, we use information provided by other organizations [insert list] including credit reference agencies. The system gives points for each piece of information that add up to produce a score. If your score reaches a certain level, we generally award credit.'

Are there any occasions when personal information need not be provided?

Some information may not have to be provided to the individual in response to a subject access request. If you decide to withhold any information, it is advisable to make a note on file in case you are challenged about this at a later date. You must only withhold information from a request if you can show that one of the exemptions under the law applies, or if the information identifies other individuals whose privacy would be jeopardized if the information were to be released.

The following are some of the commonly used exemptions from subject access requests.

- The information forms part of a negotiation process with the individual. This may include, for instance, where you are currently in negotiations with the individual regarding fees payable, a proposed reward or redundancy package or an insurance claim. If, in such cases, releasing the information you hold would prejudice negotiations, you do not have to provide it. However, if the request is made after negotiations have ceased you will have to release the information.

- The information is to be used for management forecasting and planning purposes. This could cover, for instance, the planning of an internal restructuring.

- The information contains a confidential reference that you are providing. The information will be exempt where you are the creator of such a reference but not where you are the recipient. If you receive a confidential reference (for example as a prospective employer) the individual is entitled to make a request to you to see this reference.

- Providing the information in response to a request would prejudice the detection or prevention of a particular crime.

- Providing the information in response to a request would prejudice national security.

- The information in question relates to legal advice you have received or have given as a professional legal adviser.

- Releasing the information would mean you reveal evidence of committing an offence, other than under the Data Protection Act.

- The information forms part of a health record. If you hold medical information provided by a health professional (other than yourself) on an individual, this must sometimes not be disclosed without obtaining the consent of the health professional, such as their GP, that has most recently had responsibility for the care of the individual.

Information that identifies other individuals

Where the information requested by the applicant for subject access also refers to or otherwise includes information that relates to other individuals you must take great care not to disclose their information unless absolutely necessary.

You must strike a balance between complying with the subject access requests and protecting the privacy rights of the other individuals.

You should always try to obtain the other individual's consent to the disclosure of their information. If this consent cannot be obtained it is usually preferable to avoid making a disclosure. If in doubt you should seek further legal advice rather than risk breaching the privacy rights of the other party.

For further information on exemptions, you should contact the Information Commissioner's Office. Some advice on specific exemptions is also provided in Chapter 14, *Sector-specific guidance for using personal information*.

The information won't make any sense to anyone outside my organization

Organizations will often use internal codes, abbreviations or jargon such as that used in text messages. When the information you provide in response to your subject access request contains such codes or jargon you are required to explain these, so that any individual can understand the information. You could do this by writing on the hard copy or, if such codes and abbreviations are commonly used, producing a leaflet.

I've done all the legwork – What do I do with the information now?

You have collated the information within the 40 calendar days and it is ready to be sent. Here are some final tips.

- Consider sending the information by recorded or registered delivery so that there is proof of posting and receipt. This can be helpful if there are potential issues about these dates;

- Consider refunding the £10 fee as a matter of courtesy. This may be a useful device for helping to repair any damaged customer or client relations, especially if the subject access request was prompted by a complaint about something else.

Complaints about damage and distress

I have received a letter quoting section 10 objecting to 'processing causing damage or distress' – What does this mean?

Individuals can issue a notice requiring an organization, within a reasonable time, to stop processing that is causing substantial unwarranted distress to them or to another person. The individual may object to the information being processed at all, or to some of the information being processed in a certain way. An example may be that, having failed to update your files, you are still addressing correspondence to the individual and their recently deceased partner.

You must respond within 21 calendar days as to whether:

- you have complied or intend to comply with this notice; or

- you intend to comply with part or none of the notice, giving reasons as to why, in your view, it is unjustified.

Remember that the damage or distress has to be both substantial and unwarranted. The Commissioner considers that a 'notice' from an individual could apply where the processing caused or could cause an individual to suffer loss or harm, or upset or anguish that is more than just annoyance, without justification.

Complaints about direct marketing

One of my customers has objected to direct marketing under section 11 – What do I have to do?

Individuals have the right under the Data Protection Act to object to direct marketing, i.e. marketing material that is aimed specifically at them as opposed to 'The Occupier' or 'Head of Household'.

The objection can be made at any time during or after the relationship, or even if there has never been any relationship. The Data Protection Act specifies that these requests have to be in writing, but it is generally considered good practice to handle requests made verbally too, especially if you have contacted them by telephone.

It is not necessarily as simple as removing all their details from your files. If you use lists provided by third parties, that individual could be on another list. You need a mechanism for 'flagging' up the details to show that an objection to marketing has been received.

Depending on the numbers involved, you may wish to keep a separate checklist, or develop your computer system so that some kind of 'flag' or marker will help you to identify individuals who have objected. Any subsequent marketing activity needs to be cross-checked against this list.

If you have the system or procedural capability, you could consider splitting this down by channel, for example:

- mail;
- telephone;
- email;
- fax;
- SMS (text message).

We do (and receive) business-to-business marketing – Does the Data Protection Act 1998 apply?

The Privacy and Electronic Communications Regulations cover unsolicited direct marketing by telephone to organizations as well as to individuals. You can register your organization's number with the TPS; anyone who is 'cold calling' has to screen their list against the TPS database first.

If you already have a relationship with the organization that is calling you, it will have had to explain its use of your information for direct marketing purposes to comply with the requirements of 'fair processing'. As an individual in a personal or in a business capacity (i.e. sole trader or partnership) you can object to direct marketing at this point or subsequently under the Data Protection Act. Business-to-business marketing by mail, telephone or email where there is an existing relationship is not covered by the Data Protection Act or the Privacy and Electronic Communications Regulations 2004, but as a matter of good practice the organization should respect their wishes. After all, it is a waste of time and resources to contact someone who is not interested, as well as potentially damaging to the relationship.

I have received a notice under section 12 objecting to 'automated decision-taking' – What do I do?

Individuals do not necessarily fit a particular category or type, and it may be in the interests of your relationship with that individual to bear this in mind when using an automated decision-taking process, for example to assess work performance (key stroke monitoring), creditworthiness (credit scoring) or assessment for employment (CV scanning or psychometric testing).

If the automated decision is taken for the purposes of considering whether to enter into, or with a view to entering into, a contract, or in the course of performing that contract, and the effect of the decision is to grant the request of the individual, or you have procedures in place that allow individuals to appeal, then your decisions are exempt from the individual's right to object. It is good practice to explain to the individual that this is the case and, in particular, to explain your appeal procedures.

If your decision is not exempt you have to tell the individual as soon as possible after the decision has been made. (Consider whether you have covered this in your privacy notice and whether that was given recently enough to be relied on.) The individual can respond to you within 21 calendar days asking for that decision to be reconsidered by a human or issue you with an objection notice at any time, regardless of whether such a decision has been made or even is intended to be made.

You must then respond within 21 calendar days, specifying what steps you are going to take to comply with the notice.

To summarize, you should factor in an appeals process when using systems to make decisions. The end decision does not have to be different, but it will take into account any relevant information that the system is not programmed to consider.

Claims for compensation

The individual is claiming they are entitled to compensation under section 13 – Is this right?

Individuals have the right to claim compensation through the courts for damage (financial or physical) caused by any breach of the Data Protection Act 1998 . The Information Commissioner is required to remain impartial and does not have powers to award compensation.

The most common scenario is that a breach such as an inaccuracy or an unauthorized disclosure will cause embarrassment, anguish or anger. An individual can claim compensation for distress caused only when they also suffered from damage. (NB These provisions are different in relation to processing for journalistic, artistic and literary purposes.)

> CASE STUDY
>
> A customer notifies you that following a relationship breakdown he has a new contact address. You are contacted by their ex-partner, who is also a customer requesting a forwarding address for some mail. You duly provide this in the interests of customer service. The first customer contacts you to say that the relationship broke down because of violence; the customer has had to move again and you will be picking up the bill.

There is obviously nothing to stop you making an *ex gratia* payment as a gesture of goodwill towards the individual. There is no guidance on how much this should be; factors to consider may include any costs incurred, for example telephone calls or postage or whether you consider the relationship to be worth a certain amount in monetary or goodwill terms.

If the individual is suggesting they are likely to take further action, you may wish to refer them to the Information Commissioner. They have the right to complain to the Commissioner about a breach of the Data Protection Act. It is worth bearing in mind that the Commissioner will be looking at the breach and subsequent steps to rectify this and to prevent a recurrence, not at how much money has been paid to the individual as a consolatory gesture.

Court orders for blocking, erasure and destruction

The individual claims they have a right under section 14 to have information rectified, blocked, erased or destroyed – What do I have to do?

This is a right that the individual has to exercise through the courts. It makes sense to seek a resolution to any issues long before this becomes a costly and time-consuming reality.

It is important to remember that you are obliged, under the 'accuracy principle', to note where appropriate the individual's view that information is inaccurate, even where you do not agree with this assertion.

In the event that the individual or you are looking to terminate a relationship following difficulties, you may be asked to remove everything that is on file about them. Do you need to continue processing personal information, or will anonymous information meet your needs? It may not if:

- you have any statutory obligations to hold information for a certain time, for example for tax purposes or money laundering regulations; or

- you are looking to ensure that there is no further contact with the individual, for example marketing, as you may subsequently acquire their details through another third party. In this case, explain why you need to continue processing their information, and any relevant timescales.

Chapter 10 – Employer and employee information

The Data Protection Act refers to 'individuals' regardless of what your relationship with them is. There is a danger that data protection obligations tend to be thought of in the context of a commercial relationship only, therefore forgetting the individuals about whom the most sensitive and personal complex information is stored – employees.

Using employee data

As an employer you must comply with the Data Protection Act when processing information about all your employees. This also includes information about temporary staff, volunteers and work experience students.

You must comply with all eight of the data protection principles when processing personal information about your employees.

Personal information must be processed fairly and lawfully and must be processed only for specified and compatible purposes

You must always make it clear to employees how you intend to use their information. You can do this up front by issuing a privacy notice wherever you collect employee or prospective employee information.

The following are just a few examples of where privacy notices could be issued to employees:

- at the bottom of a job application form: explaining how the information will be used and what will be done with rejected applications and the information provided on them;

- in the contract of employment: explaining how the employee's information will be used during the period of employment;

- on sick forms: explaining how the information will be used and gaining consent for the use of any sensitive health information;

- on equal opportunities monitoring forms: explaining what will become of the information and, if necessary obtaining consent;

- where monitoring of employees is to be carried out, via call recording or CCTV, for example, a notice explaining why the monitoring is occurring and what any recorded information will be used for should be provided to the employees. There may be occasions where monitoring of calls or emails may be permissible without the employee's knowledge but legal advice should be sought before carrying out any covert monitoring.

Case study

In 2009, the Information Commissioner seized a database that had been unlawfully used to vet employees and contractors working in the construction industry.

Employers from the major construction firms shared details of troublesome employees and trade union activists essentially 'blacklisting' them and preventing them from obtaining future employment. Employees were not told about the database and could not exercise their right of subject access to the information held.

The Information Commissioner has announced his intention to prosecute the operator of the database and to take action against the employers that unfairly shared data without notifying their employees.

Personal information must be accurate, up to date, relevant and not excessive and must be retained for no longer than necessary

Make sure that you retain proper employee records and avoid recording personal opinions about employees that you cannot justify. Make sure that you do not collect information about employees that is excessive or irrelevant. Be particularly careful with pre-employment vetting; do not collect or use information that has no direct relevance to the prospective employee's new job.

Personal information must be processed in accordance with the individual's rights in relation to their information

Do not forget that employees, as well as your customers and clients, have rights in relation to their personal information.

They will have access to any information you process in relation to them. This will not just include access to personal files but may also include access to the content of emails about them and confidential references that you have received from third parties. Some employers are reluctant to extend such rights to employees; however, employers have no choice in the matter because the rights are prescribed under the law. If you are worried about such access, make sure that you and your staff do not record any information about employees that could be used against you in an Industrial Tribunal, and advise third parties that provide references that their contents cannot be kept confidential.

If you use employee information for marketing purposes always allow them the option of refusing this use of their information.

Be sensitive to employees who argue that your processing of their information is causing unwarranted damage and distress.

Personal information must be kept secure and must not be transferred outside the EEA without adequate protection

Information security is absolutely paramount in the workplace. Employee records and information relate to people known within your organization. A quick glance or an overheard conversation could result in that information being disclosed, with serious repercussions for the individuals concerned. Your employees have a right to have their information protected.

Communications between an employee and a human resources professional attract a duty of confidence. Any breach of such confidence will also be a breach of data protection law.

Looking up employee information on social networking sites

There have been several stories in the press recently about employers taking action against employees because of evidence of inappropriate behaviour published on Facebook or similar social networking sites. In reality an employer that wishes to discipline an employee on the basis of pictures or comments published on their Facebook page would find this extremely difficult to accomplish lawfully unless the employee had consented to the use of this information for employment purposes.

Similarly employers that look up employees' details on the web and then use this information to make employment decisions must take great care to ensure that the information is processed fairly and lawfully. Information on the web may often be inaccurate or misleading and on its own should not be used to make important decisions about existing or potential employees.

The Employment Code of Practice

In recognition of the fact that within the human resources arena there is a plethora of other law to cross-reference when looking at data protection, coupled with the fact that there had been many complaints in this area in the past, the Information Commissioner issued a code of practice on privacy in the workplace. The code is published in four sections:

1. recruitment and selection;

2. employment records;

3. monitoring at work;

4. medical information.

Each section contains the Information Commissioner's interpretation of the legal requirements, along with good practice advice. If you are worried about the use of employee information you can download these guides free of charge from the Information Commissioner's website.

The Information Commissioner has also published a guide entitled *Monitoring at work* especially for small businesses.

Staff training in data protection: their liability (and yours)

If staff do not understand their responsibility to act in accordance with the organization's procedures and use information for their own purposes, they can be found guilty of a criminal offence. You could be breaching the Data Protection Act by failing to ensure that this is the case. You must therefore ensure that all your staff understand what is required of them in relation to the processing of personal information.

A free training DVD on the Data Protection Act and how to handle and protect people's information, *The Lights Are On*, is available from the Information Commissioner's Office.

CASE STUDY

A computer operator working for Gwent Police, in what was described as 'foolishness and boredom', looked up the records of four of her friends. It is a criminal offence to use personal information without the consent of the person in charge of the records on which it is held. She was ordered to pay £400 and £50 costs and was suspended from her job pending disciplinary proceedings.

Staff training can also be used to inform staff about their own rights under the law. This is a fantastic opportunity to raise data protection awareness. If staff understand how their own information is processed and what their rights are within the workplace, they are more likely to apply this knowledge to your relationships with other individuals.

Chapter 11 – E-commerce

Data protection law and the internet

Both the Data Protection Act and special data protection rules set out in the Privacy and Electronic Communications Regulations 2004 place obligations on organizations that use email, SMS text messages, MMS multimedia messages (pictures) or the web to contact clients and customers.

Websites

The eight data protection principles apply in full to personal information processed via a website.

Publishing personal information on a website

A court case in the European Court of Justice confirmed that publishing personal information on the internet is processing and is covered by data protection law such as the Data Protection Act.

When collecting information for publication on the internet, always make sure that the individuals who are providing their information know that it will be published in this way. If they complain that the publication may cause them damage and distress you should avoid publishing that information.

If you would like to publish sensitive personal information on the internet, you will need any individuals whose details are to be published to explicitly consent to the publication.

> ### CASE STUDY
>
> In 2003 the European Court of Justice heard the case of Mrs Lindqvist, a parishioner from Alseda, Sweden. Mrs Lindqvist was a volunteer at her local church. She had recently taken a course in website design and set up her own website to support other parishioners preparing

for confirmation. She posted information about herself on the website as well as information relating to 18 other colleagues including their names, jobs, hobbies, telephone numbers and medical data.

Mrs Lindqvist failed to inform her colleagues about this and did not ask for consent before processing the sensitive health information. Her colleagues complained and she was forced to shut down the website. She was also prosecuted for criminal offences under Swedish data protection law. She was convicted of processing personal data by automatic means without notifying the Swedish data protection authorities. Mrs Lindqvist appealed against her conviction on the grounds that publishing the information on the web was not 'processing' the information.

However, the court did not uphold her appeal and found that making reference to living individuals on the web, as she had done, amounted to the processing of personal information.

Even if you are only publishing information on a company intranet, rather than the publicly available internet, the same rules apply, although you should explain to the individual that access to their information will be limited to those individuals who can access the intranet.

CASE STUDY

In 2002, the Information Commissioner investigated the case of a trade union employee who pursued a grievance with his employer about bullying in the workplace. The employee took time off sick as a result of the bullying. The details of the employee's grievance and his illness were discussed at meetings, the minutes of which were published on the trade union's website. The employee was not informed of the publication.

The Information Commissioner found that a breach of the Data Protection Act 1998 requirement that processing be fair and lawful had occurred.

Is publishing personal data on the web a transfer outside the EEA?

As personal information that is published on the internet can be accessed anywhere in the world, it was once thought that the rules relating to transfer of data outside the EEA applied to such publications. However, in the Lindqvist case the European Court of Justice found that this was not the case.

The ruling applies across the EEA and as a result organizations in the UK publishing on the internet do not have to comply with the rules relating to transfer of personal information set out in the eighth principle of the Data Protection Act 1998 as long as their server infrastructure is based within the EU.

Collection of information over the internet

If you use your website to collect any personal information, even just email addresses, you must provide a privacy notice as usual. You are also advised to post a privacy policy on the website explaining in more detail exactly how you use the information and perhaps to provide information about the person in the organization who can be contacted in relation to any concerns about how the information is processed.

You can take the pain out of the process of drafting your own privacy policy by using an automatic privacy policy generator such as that provided by the Organization for Economic Co-operation and Development (OECD) (recommended by and developed with the help of the UK Information Commissioner).

Five things to consider including in your privacy policy

There are five things to consider including in your privacy policy:

1. your standard privacy notice;

2. a high level description of any security measures that you have put in place to safeguard personal information provided via your website;

3. whether or not you use any cookies or similar devices to collect information, what information they collect and what it is to be used for;

4. information and guidance about what a cookie is and how to 'switch it off' (see *Cookies, web bugs and other 'spyware'* on page 79);

5. contact details, preferably an email address, for individuals who wish to opt out of direct marketing and who wish to make a subject access request to your organization.

Using personal information collected over a website

You should only use personal information collected over the web in line with your privacy notice, notification to the Information Commissioner and the terms of your privacy policy.

Information published on social networking sites

You should avoid collecting and using information from social networking sites such as Facebook for commercial purposes unless you are sure that you can do this in a way that complies with the Data Protection Act. If you use your organization's Facebook or Twitter page to collect information about 'friends' or 'followers' to use for commercial purposes then you must make this clear in a privacy notice displayed on the page. You should also avoid collecting personal information from customer or employees' social networking pages for commercial use unless you have obtained their agreement to this.

Cookies, web bugs and other 'spyware'

What are cookies and web bugs?

Cookies, web bugs and other similar technologies are often referred to as 'spyware'. They are software components and programmes that are transferred from websites to an individual's computer terminal when that individual visits the website.

The software then records or enables the website to record information about the individual web user's navigation around the website, for example, the web pages they visit, hyperlinks followed or online advertisements that the visitor accesses. In some cases the information collected can be considered to be personal information, particularly where an individual has also provided their email address or other details to the website and the website matches this with the navigation information.

Using spyware technologies such as cookies is not prohibited by data protection law, but where personal information is collected using such technology, data protection law will apply. Both the Data Protection Act 1998 and the Privacy and Electronic Communications Regulations 2004 have implications for the way in which such spyware can be used. The following is a summary of the rules.

- Avoid using spyware to collect personal information, i.e. do not attempt to match navigation information such as browsing habits with the individual's email address, name or other identifying data.

- Where such technologies are used to collect personal information make website visitors aware of this via privacy notices, provided either via your privacy policy, or preferably via pop up boxes before the technology is employed. Be clear about the ways in which the information being collected and stored by spyware will be used and how the individual can access the information being collected.

- Provide individuals visiting your website with the opportunity to reject the use of spyware and inform them of this right via your privacy policy.

How to inform web visitors of their right to reject spyware

If information about the right to reject spyware is provided via a privacy policy then links to the policy should be provided on the homepage or wherever a visitor enters the site.

Guidance on explaining cookies and their uses is provided by the Interactive Advertising Bureau (IAB). Its website is a useful source of information, and you can also provide a link from your privacy policy direct to its website free of charge.

You can ask the individual to take action to turn off the spyware, but if you take this route you must explain how they can do this by using clear non-technical instructions.

What if the spyware is essential to the operation of the site or the provision of the service?

If the services you provide through your website rely on cookies or spyware to ensure they function properly, for example to provide an electronic shopping basket that remembers the goods an on-line shopper has bought, you do not have to offer visitors to the site a chance to refuse such cookies. However, if you wish to rely on this argument you must be able to show that the use of the cookies is 'strictly necessary', and you should not continue to collect or store information using cookies or other spyware once the activity or service they support is complete.

Marketing on the web

Marketing via the internet is covered by the Data Protection Act and individuals can exercise their right to object to direct marketing carried out over the web, at any time. You are also required to explain clearly in your privacy notice to individuals that their email address, telephone number or other contact details may be used for marketing.

Email, SMS text and MMS multimedia messages

The Privacy and Electronic Communications Regulations 2004 set out even more stringent criteria for the use of email, SMS and MMS for marketing.

It will usually not be enough just to tell individuals that their information will be used in this way. Instead, you will usually be required to gain their informed consent to market them by email, SMS or MMS.

This means that they must actively agree, for example by ticking a box or indicating their verbal agreement, before you can market them in this way.

The only exception to this is where the following three conditions are fulfilled:

1. you collected their email address or telephone number in the course of a sale or negotiations for a sale of a product or service;

2. you limit your marketing to the marketing of similar products or services to those originally sold; and

3. in each communication you give the individual the means to object, free of charge, to receiving any more marketing communications via the medium in question.

This is known as marketing on a 'soft' opt-in basis.

Contact details

Regardless of whether or not you have obtained the individual's consent to full marketing or are proceeding to market them in the limited way described above on a soft opt-in basis, you must also always provide the individual with the following details each time you send them a marketing communication. You must:

- always provide an address to which they can respond to opt out of receiving any further marketing (this can be an email address); and

- always make clear your identity as the sender; never make any attempt to conceal or disguise your identity.

Such contact information must be included in every communication regardless of whether the marketing message is sent by SMS, MMS or email.

SMS and MMS may present particular problems as the screens to which the communications are sent may be small and the number of characters limited. Nevertheless, the law must still be followed.

Taking payments over the web

If you take credit card payments over the web, you will need to ensure that there is adequate security for the data. There could be serious consequences if your website is designed in a way that allows hackers to access credit card information to use for fraudulent purposes. APACS is the UK's trade association for the payment card industry, and anyone processing credit card payments over the web must comply with its standards.

Chapter 12 – Operating a CCTV system

Many small businesses use CCTV to protect their premises or business. However, the implementation of a video or video and audio surveillance system such as this can raise serious security concerns.

In many cases, CCTV may record personal information from which individuals are easily recognizable. If your CCTV system records images or audio data from which individuals can be recognized or identified then you will need to ensure that your CCTV system complies with the law.

Basic rules for operating a CCTV system

Establish whether your use of CCTV can be justified

You must ensure that the collection and use of any images or other personal information you record using CCTV can be justified on the basis of your legitimate business interests or other grounds (see Chapter 4, *Collecting personal information*, and Chapter 5, *Using personal information*, for details).

Because of the invasive nature of CCTV, it is advisable to carry out a privacy impact assessment (see Chapter 5, *Using personal information*) to ensure that you can justify its use.

In most cases, you will be using CCTV to protect your business and you must ensure that the use of the system is proportionate to the risk posed to your business. For example, it may be perfectly justifiable to use CCTV inside a shop to monitor and deter potential shoplifters, but it would be unlikely to be acceptable to use the same CCTV system to monitor whether your own staff members were working hard enough.

The use of the CCTV system to monitor shoplifting would be likely to be legitimate as there is a serious risk posed to your business from theft. However, issues such as staff productivity could easily be monitored and addressed by other means, for example by more effective management supervision, rather than by video surveillance, which the staff may feel invades their privacy.

Where you use CCTV is an issue that may also affect the outcome of your privacy impact assessment. The use of CCTV in bathrooms, sunbed salon cubicles or even in areas such as doctors' surgeries would be regarded as potentially more of a risk to privacy than the use of such systems in public areas such as the street or a reception area.

Notification

If you do implement a CCTV system you must ensure that you notify the uses and ways in which you process any personal information collected through it in your notification to the Information Commissioner. The most commonly cited purposes for using CCTV systems is for crime prevention and detection.

Privacy notices

If you routinely use CCTV in an area, you should ensure that you provide clear signage throughout the area explaining that it is in operation, what the CCTV is being used for and contact details for the operator.

Using CCTV data for other purposes

If you want to use images from a CCTV system designed to collect personal information for one purpose for another unrelated purpose you need to check whether this will be allowable under the Data Protection Act.

Some additional uses may be allowable. For example, if the CCTV footage records images that can be used to help prevent and detect crime or images that may be useful in a civil legal dispute, then such further use may be allowed. However, in general it will not be possible to use the footage or recording for different purposes from those notified to people via the signage.

It would not usually, for example, be acceptable to use footage from a CCTV system installed to prevent vandalism and crime to:

- monitor employees at work and reprimand them for poor performance or unprofessional behaviour;

- record funny or interesting events to publish on the internet or to provide to a TV show;

- use recordings for future staff training, without first gaining the staff's agreement.

Quality issues and CCTV data

Your CCTV system should operate effectively and should be capable of recording images that are of an appropriate quality for the purposes for which you need to use it.

For instance, the quality should be good enough to allow you to make an accurate identification of criminals if this is its primary purpose. If your CCTV includes date stamping, this must be set accurately so that the correct images can be related to the time in question.

Positioning the cameras

You should only seek to collect relevant images using your CCTV system. You should position your cameras to cover only the places that are under surveillance. They should not be focused on wider areas or you will risk collecting irrelevant information that you do not need.

In particular, make sure that your cameras do not inadvertently record images of domestic premises such as front gardens or through the windows of domestic dwellings. Always check the positioning of the cameras to make sure you avoid this. If your cameras are recording in areas where there are a lot of domestic dwellings you should consider using fixed rather than moveable cameras to avoid the risk of a member of staff repositioning a camera to look at domestic premises.

Access rights to CCTV data

If you record and keep images of identifiable individuals, they may ask for a copy of the recording under their right of subject access. You will need to be able to provide a copy of the tape for them. In some cases you may have to edit out or blur the features of other individuals who appear in the recording in order not to jeopardize their privacy. There are specialist firms that can do this for you.

Retaining CCTV data

You should only retain CCTV recordings for the minimum time necessary to fulfil your business purpose. In many cases you may only need access to CCTV footage in 'real time' and may not need to make any recording at all. If you do need to keep CCTV recordings, always retain them securely and ensure that you destroy them securely so that they can no longer be viewed. A technique called 'degaussing' can be used to achieve this permanent deletion.

Sharing CCTV data with other organizations

Law enforcement agencies such as the police may sometimes need access to CCTV data. You should treat this in the same way as you would any other request for personal information. You should follow the steps set out for sharing information with the police in the *FAQs* in Chapter 7, *Disclosing and sharing personal information*, page 42.

CCTV Code of Practice

The Information Commissioner's Office has published a very useful document, *CCTV Code of Practice*, which covers the use of CCTV in spaces that are open to the public such as shops, reception areas and streets. The Code is available from the Information Commissioner's website.

Chapter 13 – Security and disposal of personal information

This chapter covers the seventh data protection principle:

7. Personal information must be kept secure.

Security

The Data Protection Act makes you responsible for ensuring the security of the personal information you process, but putting in place good security to protect personal information benefits you as well as your customers or clients.

Information on individuals is a valuable asset. It enables you to create, maintain and build customer and client relationships. These relationships are often dependent on trust and an expectation of confidentiality.

Unfortunately, as with any other valuable asset, the personal information you process may attract the intention of less scrupulous organizations and individuals. This might result in attacks on your technical and organizational systems and processes.

Such attacks might take the form of technical assaults, for example 'hackers' from inside and outside your organization trying to gain access to IT systems, or less sophisticated but effective attempts at 'information blagging', i.e. individuals tricking your staff into disclosing personal information.

The following are examples of technical attacks:

- use of Trojan horses and viruses that pass information back to the hacker;
- exploitation of security 'back doors' in systems;
- ex-employees using old passwords to gain access;
- existing employees with unrestricted access straying into databases and systems they should be prevented from reaching.

The following are examples of common 'information blagging' practices:

- the attacker pretends to be the individual who is entitled to the information;

- the attacker persuades a member of your staff that they are acting on behalf of the individual;

- the attacker pretends to be a lawyer, police officer, employer or government official who has the authority to access information;

- in a larger organization an external attacker may pretend to be calling from another department within the organization requesting information.

The following are the threats that have arisen as a result of technical attacks 'or information blagging' practices:

- identity theft, which is the fastest growing crime in the UK. Criminals will look to gather as much information as possible about an individual so that they can impersonate them to obtain money and property;

- partners, in particular in the context of a relationship breakdown. Information on a partner's financial affairs and daily transactions can be useful in financial settlements;

- private investigators and tracing agents paid to obtain personal information;

- employees using your information for their own purposes.

Further information about 'information blagging' is available from the Information Commissioner's Office.

Damage to reputation

Allowing a breach of security to occur can seriously damage your relationship with customers or clients.

Imagine how you would feel if someone fraudulently obtained credit in your name, your new address details were disclosed to a violent ex-partner or associate, your bank account details were found in a council skip or your medical details were overheard by a neighbour? These are some of the potential consequences if those organizations you have a relationship with, whether either in a professional or personal capacity, did not have adequate security measures in place.

If it is a crime, why am I responsible?

Obtaining, disclosing or offering to disclose information contrary to your organization's procedures is a criminal offence under the Data Protection Act. Computer hacking is also a criminal offence under the Computer Misuse Act 1990.

However, this alone is not a deterrent, which is why you have to be on your guard to protect the confidential information entrusted to you. The Information Commissioner will not hold you responsible for being the victim of a criminal attack unless he believes that the security measures you have in place are not appropriate. If they are found not to have been appropriate, the Information Commissioner could find you in breach of the law allowing individuals who have suffered damage as the result of any security breach to claim compensation directly from you.

It is therefore very important to ensure that any security measures you do take are appropriate.

Which security measures?

The Data Protection Act requires that you put in place appropriate technical and organizational security safeguards. Unfortunately, it contains little detail about what security measures are actually required. This book is not a book about information security, but this chapter includes some very basic tips on protecting personal data. If you need detailed advice on security measures you should refer to the BS ISO 27001 series of standards which contain detailed guidance. These are available from BSI.

When evaluating what level of security is appropriate you should consider what solutions are available and their cost, weighed up against the level of harm that may result from an unauthorized disclosure or if this information was lost or corrupted in some way – a 'risk-based approach'. Consider whether:

- the information is confidential or sensitive;
- you would lose the individual's trust/confidence/business as a consequence of a security breach;
- the loss of data would affect your ability to continue the relationship;
- this information would be useful outside your organization;
- you would suffer financial loss or loss of reputation (goodwill payments or possible compensation claims through the courts).

You must take reasonable steps to ensure the reliability of your staff who have access to the personal information (for example, pre-employment checks, training) and if you use an outsourcer, that there is a contract in place with them requiring them to also have adequate security measures and to act only on your instructions, as you are responsible for their processing. There is more information on this later in this chapter.

A bank employee was prosecuted under the Data Protection Act 1998 for looking up the financial details of his former father-in-law and making him aware that he had done so. The Information Commissioner investigated following a complaint from the bank's customer and, satisfied that the bank had adequate training procedures in place, did not take any further action against the bank.

Technical measures

Personal information held on a PC, laptop, palmtop or similar devices can be rapidly disclosed to a large number of people unless proper technical security measures are put in place. It can also be at threat from technical and organizational problems. Encryption is now the accepted method for protecting such data. The Information Commissioner has recently taken action against companies that fail to protect personal data by encryption.

At the very least your organization should try to ensure that all laptops that hold personal data have encrypted hard drives and that staff are only allowed to download personal data to removable media such as USB drives and CD-ROMS where these are encrypted.

In 2008, the Information Commissioner found Virgin Media Limited in breach of the Data Protection Act following the loss of an unencrypted CD containing the personal details of over 3,000 customers.

The company signed a formal undertaking to comply with the principles of the Act, and going forwards both it and any outsourcers acting on its behalf are required to ensure all portable or mobile devices that store personal information are encrypted.

Even where computers are encrypted, the encryption will only be as good as the passwords used to lock the systems; any encryption system that is implemented should also be backed up by adequate password and access controls.

Orange Personal Communications Limited signed a formal undertaking in 2007 after an investigation by the Information Commissioner revealed that new members of staff were allowed to share user names and passwords when accessing the company IT system.

Such a process would not enable an effective audit trail in the event that an accusation concerning the processing (and potential misuse) of personal information is made.

Table 1 contains some suggestions for technical security measures that you can put in place within your organization.

Table 1 — Technical security measures

What?	How?	When?
Access rights	Access to the organization's system(s), for example customer databases or correspondence, should be granted on a 'need to know' basis, in order for an employee to perform their job	Consider regular reviews, at a minimum when there are job changes and staff members leave
Passwords	Will ensure only authorized individuals can access the system as long as they are not 'WEAK' – not *written* down, not *easily* guessed, not *anyone's* for the use of and not *kept* too long. A system prompt could help here	Where one or more computer applications are used by two or more staff
Screen savers	Set a PC to display a screen saver after a certain period of inaction and it will hide the contents of your screen	Useful in spaces open to the public
Audit trails	Track who has accessed what, and when	Useful where subsequent checks need to be made following an unauthorized disclosure, or where there is a dispute with an individual
Encryption	If you are regularly transferring information to an external third party, for example a supplier or customer, you may wish to consider installing encryption technology	Important where the personal information is sensitive, or it is commercially sensitive

Table 1 — *Technical security measures* (continued)

What?	How?	When?
BS 7799	Is a security standard accredited by and adopted by the International Organization for Standardization. It comprises ten sections: 1. security policy; 2. security organization; 3. assets clarification and control; 4. personnel security; 5. physical and environmental security; 6. communication and operations management; 7. access control; 8. systems development and maintenance; 9. business continuity management; 10. compliance checking. Part 2 and Part 3 have also been published. See BSI's website for further information.	Accreditations included on company information; viewed favourably if tendering for business
CCTV	Used as a deterrent and as evidence in relation to a criminal investigation. A code of practice has been published by the Information Commissioner.	You have areas accessible by the public or to protect your property against crime
Call recording	To record digitally or on tape the contents of a conversation for future reference	As a back-up on order lines
Firewall	To ensure that information is secure within an environment, only allows entry to authorized information from the internet.	You have branches in different locations

Table 1 — Technical security measures (continued)

What?	How?	When?
Antivirus software	If Trojan horses and worms sound like something from a strange children's zoo, it's time to take action. Computer viruses can vary from displaying annoying messages to ultimately wiping files from your system. You can protect yourself by installing antivirus software, such as scanners, to detect and eliminate viruses; such software has to be regularly updated to detect the latest viruses; subscription to an email alert service makes you aware of the latest viruses and software to protect against them	You use the internet regularly and download software or games
Back-up data	Use encrypted floppy disks or CD-ROMs to back up information on a regular basis (consider how often it is changed). Consider storing these in a different but safe place	Having a back-up will ensure continuity in the event of a disaster
Websites	Investigate and invest in technology to prevent information being intercepted, for example, Trust-e	Where you have data capture forms online

Organizational measures

CASE STUDY

In 2007, 11 banks and financial institutions, as well as the Post Office, were made to sign a formal undertaking by the Information Commissioner after confidential personal information was found in bins outside their premises. The Immigration Advisory Service was also found to have disposed of personal information in a similar way.

Of the breach, the Information Commissioner's Office said, 'It is vital that banks and other organizations take security seriously. If they do not, they not only risk further action from the Information Commissioner but also risk losing the trust of their customers. Individuals must feel confident that banks and other organizations are safeguarding their personal information.'

Table 2 contains some suggestions for organizational security measures that you can put in place within your organization.

*Table 2 — **Organizational security measures***

What?	How?	When?
Identification and verification	Procedures for outbound and inbound calls or face-to-face meetings to identify and verify the identity of the individual. Bear in mind on outbound calls where you are contacting the individual on a number they have specifically provided for that purpose, there is a lesser risk of disclosing to an unauthorized third party **Incoming calls:** • Ask for full name, address, postcode and date of birth. Depending on the nature of the relationship and the personal information you hold, you may decide to go one step further and ask the individual to provide information that would only be known to them, for example date of last visit/appointment or details of last order • If in any doubt, do not disclose any information, even if accused of 'bad customer service'. Where appropriate, offer to post information to the address held on record. A genuine customer will appreciate the measures taken to safeguard their personal information. It is a good idea to make a note on file if you suspect an unauthorized access attempt in order to make other staff aware	Where you do not automatically recognize the face or voice of an individual

*Table 2 — **Organizational security measures** (continued)*

What?	How?	When?
Identification and verification	**Outbound calls:** • Ask for the full name. You may want to ask further questions if the content of your call is going to reveal an existing relationship, for example, 'As an existing customer...' It is also prudent to check that there is only one person of that name at that address – fathers and sons can often have the same name In the light of increasing awareness about identity theft and fraud, you may receive some resistance to providing information to you where individuals believe that you may not be who you say you are, especially where there is no existing relationship between you. Failure to make security checks, however, can also undermine how the individual perceives you and your organization	Where you do not automatically recognize the face or voice of an individual
Leaving messages	If absolutely necessary, leave a message, give your name, organization and telephone number but no message (other than 'please call back'). Leaving the name of the organization does not necessarily imply there is a relationship should a third party pick up the message. Not leaving the organization's name can be taken to imply that there is a relationship of a different kind	Avoid leaving messages on answer phones and voice-mail where possible as you are unaware who may pick up these messages

Table 2 — Organizational security measures (continued)

What?	How?	When?
Access to your building	Ask the leaseholder or management agent to put in place security measures, such as keypads, at all main entrances and at entrances to separate units. Ask whether security provisions, such as nominated key holders and disclosure of the alarm code, can be incorporated into the requirements of the lease	Where your building is shared
	Consider a reception desk or have procedures to ensure that strangers are greeted on entrance	Where your organization occupies the whole building
	Visitors should sign in and be escorted around the building during their stay. Minimize risk by ensuring that as much personal information as possible is out of sight. Although this may not give the true 'flavour' of life in your organization, explain your approach to confidentiality. This is more likely to gain support from a potential supplier, client or backer	Where you have external visitors to the premises, including open days
Clear desk policy	Consider that even staff within the organization should only have access on a 'need to know' basis	At the end of each working day as a minimum
Confidential waste	Separate confidential waste from general waste. As a rule of thumb, treat it as your own information. Buy shredders from a stationer or outsource to a confidential waste company (but do not forget your outsourcing obligations)	Criminals target rubbish for personal information to use to obtain goods and money by deception
Fireproof cabinets	Ensure that business critical information, such as insurance documents and key contacts, is stored in fireproof cabinets when not in use	Ensures business continuity in the event of a disaster

*Table 2 — **Organizational security measures** (continued)*

What?	How?	When?
Staff	Who works for you? When employing staff it is good practice, from both a data protection and commercial point of view, to ensure that checks are made and references are sought Contact the Criminal Records Bureau for information on checks you can conduct on prospective employees	Do not forget you are entrusting this individual with one of your organization's most valuable assets
Training	Staff should undergo training when they begin their new job, and regularly after that (annually is commonly regarded as good practice). Your approach should take into consideration the nature of their jobs. What type of information will they be dealing with in their role? Will they be retrained if they move to another role with different responsibilities? Also consider the most effective and practical way of delivering this training bearing in mind geographical location, numbers, and business commitments, for example manning the phones. Some options are: • classroom-based presentation or workshop; • online computer-based training package; • reading materials; • videos Consider the personal information you use when carrying out training. Would your customers appreciate being renamed after a famous celebrity? Or worse, something derogatory? Changing contact details has obvious repercussions.	Training procedures can act as a defence should an individual commit a criminal offence Training on systems or operational procedures

Table 2 — *Organizational security measures* (continued)

What?	How?	When?
	Consider whether it is possible to create a specific training database or dummy files for practice. If not, record a sample number of files onto a disk so these can be used outside the live environment	
Information on the road	Where possible, avoid leaving information in hotel rooms or visible in a vehicle. Minimize the amount of information stored on the hard drive of your laptop and ensure that its hard drive is encrypted, in case it falls into the wrong hands

Think before using a mobile phone in public places, especially when giving out your own or an individual's information; you do not know who may be listening | The requirement to take security measures extends beyond the four walls of the organization. It may be necessary to take personal information with you, whether on a laptop, files or even an appointments diary, 'on the road' or to work on at home. Extra care is needed in those situations |
| Call monitoring | Ensure that your call scripts and literature include a notification to individuals, for example, 'calls may be monitored for training and quality control purposes' | To identify training needs and to ensure that procedures are being adhered to, listen in to calls periodically using an additional headset |

Other things to remember

Don't mix business with pleasure out of the office. Avoid the temptation to discuss personal information (and commercially sensitive information) with colleagues in public areas such as hotel bars, waiting areas or even the local pub or restaurant.

If your staff members regularly work from home, there are obviously data protection considerations in addition to health and safety, insurance and tax. Some points to consider are:

- providing computer equipment (hardware and software) and a telephone line specifically and only for business use. Policies should set out that any organizational data or bespoke organizational software is not to be copied, or additional software or hardware added;

- that the home in question has appropriate security measures (again, something the organization may look to help with);

- that any equipment or documentation is not accessed by any other member of the household.

When information has to be sent to a colleague at another office, to a supplier or another third party, you need to consider carefully the best method to use bearing in mind the nature of the information in question (see Table 3).

Table 3 — Information transfer

How?	Why?	Why not?
Hand deliver	Certainty of delivery	Geographical location may make this impossible
Email	Quick	Without additional security in place, such as encryption, it can be intercepted
Fax	Quick	One digit wrong means that a third party receives it
Telephone	Instantaneous	Information may be misheard or overheard
Mail	Slow	Can go astray. However, it is an offence to open someone else's mail
Courier	Certainty of delivery	Cost and timing

Protect yourself and your clients or customers from fraud

Good security benefits both you and the individuals whose information is being protected. It is in everyone's interest to protect personal information from fraudsters.

Fraud checklist: protect yourself and your organization

The following is a checklist of the things that you should be doing when processing information.

- Shred documents such as statements, bills and receipts.

- Check bank accounts and credit card statements regularly and query suspicious transactions with your bank.

- Obtain a copy of your credit file from the credit reference agencies to check for any credit searches or new accounts that you have not authorized.

- Close any dormant accounts.

- Contact your bank if you receive letters, faxes or emails (sometimes with an embedded link to a very plausible but fake site) asking you to disclose passwords.

- Never give information over the phone to someone who cannot prove their identity. If in doubt, ask them for their name and that of their organization and obtain a telephone number via directory enquiries to call them back. Your bank will not ask you to divulge account information over the phone or by email; be very wary of anyone who does.

- Never disclose or write down your PINs or passwords. Doing this may contravene the terms and conditions of the account.

- Check that documents have arrived on time. When did you receive your last statement? Fraudsters often set up false mail redirections.

- Inform the relevant companies if information has gone astray.

- Limit the amount of information you carry around in case your bag/briefcase/car is stolen.

- Keep a note of credit card numbers with account numbers and emergency telephone numbers; in the event of having to report your cards stolen, time is of the essence.

- Do not carry all your credit cards around with you.

- When giving personal information on the web, check for the padlock symbol at the bottom of the page.

- Ensure that your rubbish is properly disposed of to avoid being the victim of 'dumpster diving' by criminals who will target commercial and residential addresses in certain areas to collect personal information to sell on, or to use themselves in 'identity theft'.

Outsourcing

Data processors

To meet the growing needs of your organization you may decide to use a third party or 'outsourcer' to undertake some work on your behalf. Where this involves personal information, there are some key considerations, as you remain liable if there is a breach of the Data Protection Act.

- Does the outsourcer have security measures in place that are similar to yours? Ask the outsourcer to complete a self-assessment checklist for review. Considering the nature of the data (for example, contact details or sensitive personal data) and the frequency of processing (regular activity or a one-off contract?), you may wish to verify this with a visit.

- There must be a contract in place which specifies that the outsourcer acts only on your instructions (including approval of any further subcontracting relationships); you have the right to check adequate security measures are in place.

What if it goes wrong?

Any enforcement or prosecution action for breaching the Data Protection Act will be against you as you are responsible for the processing of personal information by your outsourcer. You then have the option of taking civil action against your outsourcer for breach of contract, to recover costs such as fines, compensation paid to individuals and compensation for damage to reputation.

I am a data processor – What are my obligations?

Unless you also process information in your own right as an organization, you will have no obligations under the Data Protection Act as the organization (the 'data controller') is responsible for all your processing, and is liable if you get it wrong.

You have to demonstrate that you comply with the same security measures in the Data Protection Act as any other organization although, for you, this will be a contractual requirement rather than a statutory requirement. These security measures include:

- having adequate security measures in place;

- ensuring that your staff are reliable by making pre-employment checks and training them;

- acting only on the instructions of the organization you are working for.

In addition, if you work for more than one client, you will have to ensure that you have procedures in place to keep their data separate.

They have a responsibility to keep a check on your compliance, and it is in their interests to give you guidance. Ultimately they could take action against you for breach of contract.

If you do some work in your own right as an organization, you will have to comply with all the requirements of the Data Protection Act.

Disposal and destruction of personal information

There are no rules set out in data protection law that deal with the exact requirements for the destruction of personal information, although the general requirements in relation to security will apply.

If you no longer have any need to retain personal information then it should be completely deleted from your computer systems and manual records should be shredded or incinerated.

When deleting information from your computer systems, you should be aware that pressing the delete button may not be sufficient. As far as possible you should erase the data so that it cannot be recovered.

REMEMBER

When disposing of old hardware to remove the hard drives before disposal. Hard drives should be destroyed so that the data they hold cannot be recovered. Resist the temptation to sell on old computers or to donate them to charity without first ensuring that the hard drive has been removed. It may not be enough to merely 'wipe' the hard drive clean of data unless you use a specialist firm.

CASE STUDY

In February 2000, *The Guardian* newspaper reported that the ex-Beatle Sir Paul McCartney's banking details were found on the hard drive of a PC that had been owned by Morgan Grenfell Asset Management. The PC had been decommissioned and given to a third party; however, the memory on the hard drive had not been effectively erased. It was therefore possible to recover client details from the machine.

You should also ensure that any other medium used to store personal information is disposed of in a secure manner when it is no longer needed. Remember to dispose of the following items safely and securely as the personal data they hold could be recovered:

- tape used for call recording and CCTV;
- printer ribbons;
- floppy discs and CD-ROMs;
- computer printouts.

Some tips for introducing work practices that help to ensure secure disposal of personal data include using:

- a shredder;

- special bags for confidential paper waste;

- special bins for old electronic media such as floppy discs and CDs;

- a specialist waste disposal firm that can provide certificates of destruction.

REMEMBER

If you employ a waste disposal company to dispose of your confidential waste, make sure it does so securely. If possible you should make clear exactly how the information should be disposed of in a contract with the company.

CASE STUDY

A report in the *Information Commissioner's Annual Report* explained how a council employee alerted them to the fact that his employer had disposed of personnel information by placing the old records in black bin bags that were sent to the local tip. The information contained computer-generated printouts relating to health information. The Information Commissioner found that a breach of the Data Protection Act 1998 had occurred.

Chapter 14 – Sector-specific guidance for using personal information

Accountants, solicitors and other professionals

Accountants, solicitors and other professional people who operate under codes of conduct and industry guidelines can seriously damage their reputations if they fall foul of the Data Protection Act.

Obviously, accountants and solicitors must comply with all aspects of the Data Protection Act in their own right, but they should take particular care to avoid committing any offences under the law as this could result in them not being able to continue in their preferred career.

The most common offences committed by professionals usually relate to the illegal obtaining of information either as a result of 'removing client information' from an ex-employer in order to set up a rival business or, particularly for solicitors, using a third party, such as a private detective, to obtain information in an illegal way.

Avoid these two serious errors by ensuring that you always understand who owns the client information and what rights you have over it when leaving a firm, and take precautions when hiring others by checking their past records and placing restrictions upon them to collect information by lawful means.

Consultants

Consultants who provide management or IT consultancy advice to other organizations often have access to personal information belonging to those other organizations. However, in most cases such a relationship will be governed by a contract under which the consultant is obliged to meet data protection requirements.

In such cases, the consultant will be acting as a data processor and must comply with the terms of the contract rather than directly with the Data Protection Act. However, this will usually still mean that the consultant is required to ensure that they have an appropriate level of data protection knowledge (reading this book is a good start). In addition, consultants must never make their own uses of personal information relating to a client's customers or employees or they will risk committing a criminal offence.

Consultants will, of course, be capable of processing personal information on their own behalf during the course of running their own businesses. In particular, they must comply with requirements for notification (unless exempt), marketing, even to other businesses, and if they are employers, in relation to their employee information.

Independent financial advisers

As a financial intermediary, you are collecting personal information on behalf of yourself or both yourself and the financial service provider. Where you process personal information on your own behalf you must comply in full with all the provisions of the law.

Independent financial advisers (IFAs) are exactly that – independent. This means that you are likely to be subject to the requirements of the law in your own right, and you are unlikely to be a data processor for the financial services organizations whose products you sell.

This means you must ensure that any information you collect from clients is preceded by your own privacy notice, explaining who you are and how you will use their information.

As an IFA you are already required to provide certain notifications in order to comply with the Financial Services and Markets Act 2000. You should take the opportunity to combine your privacy notice with other notifications. But remember that your privacy notice must be provided before you collect any personal information.

You may also be asking your clients to fill in applications forms provided by other financial advisers. This information will be accompanied by the organization's own privacy notice. Make sure you familiarize yourself with this wording so that you can explain it to your customers.

Sometimes the wording might be quite alarming, as it may mention disclosures that are made to credit reference agencies and fraud databases. If you are unsure of how to describe these to your client, you should check with the financial services provider about the type of explanation you should provide.

You should always ensure that you use up-to-date information when helping a client to complete an application form. If you sell credit products you may also need to comply with some of the rules set out for credit brokers as well as any guidelines set by your regulator, the Financial Services Authority (FSA). (For more information about the FSA, see its website.)

As an IFA you are already working in a highly regulated profession and therefore should not find complying with data protection law to be a burden.

Under FSA rules, you are already required to pay due regard to the interests of your customers, to treat them fairly, to respect the information needs of your clients and to communicate information to them in a way that is clear, fair and not misleading. These requirements are not that far from those set out in the Data Protection Act.

Credit brokers

If you act as a credit broker, you help to arrange finance and leasing products for members of the public by making credit applications on their behalf.

You will have to comply with all aspects of the law when acting in this capacity (so if you have skipped to this section you will still have to read the rest of the book) but there are some issues to which you must pay special attention to avoid falling foul of the law.

A common complaint about credit brokers is that they do not make clear to customers how many applications for credit they will be making on their behalf.

This is important because if too many credit searches are listed against an individual's credit file, their credit status may be adversely affected and this may prevent them from obtaining credit in the future. The searches will remain on the customer's file for up to two years.

Before you collect the information, you must make clear which applications you will be making. You must also provide the details of the companies to whom you will be passing their information in order to progress the credit application and an explanation of how those companies will use the information. In particular you must explain that the finance companies will each separately search the customer's credit file and that records of these searches may be recorded, as well as the adverse consequences of this. Useful information on how to communicate this to customers is available from the Finance and Leasing Association's website.

Never use information that you know or suspect to be inaccurate on a customer's application or encourage the customer to mislead the credit company about their income, employment or other characteristics that might affect their credit rating, as this information could result in suspicions about the authenticity of the application and may lead to a fraud marker being placed against the customer's credit file. Always use up-to-date information and never assume that a client's details have not changed since you last did business with them.

The Finance and Leasing Association also advises checking the finance companies' application forms or websites to find their privacy notice so that you can then draw it to the attention of the customer. You can allow the customers to read this information themselves or you can read it to them.

Private investigators and tracing agents

Individuals working as private investigators and tracing agents account for almost all prosecutions under the Data Protection Act 1998 and its predecessor the Data Protection Act 1984.

These offences usually relate to the obtaining or procurement of personal information by deception or the sale of information obtained in this way.

Whilst you should, of course, ensure that you comply with all aspects of the data protection law, your main focus should be on ensuring that you always obtain information fairly and do not stray into practices that might amount to illegal activity. The following should be avoided.

- Never try to obtain information by pretending to be either the individual to whom the information relates or another person who might be entitled to the data.

- When obtaining information from associates of the individual you are tracing or investigating, do not mislead them into providing information by suggesting that you are acting for the benefit of the individual, for example by maintaining that you need to contact them because they have won a prize.

- Never offer to obtain information for someone else when you know this cannot be achieved lawfully.

- Never ask anyone else to obtain information for you using deception or unlawful means, for example asking an employee to reveal information about their employer's clients or customers.

- Never sell information that you suspect may have been obtained unlawfully.

> **REMEMBER**
>
> If you should break any of these rules you could be prosecuted for a criminal offence, fined and prevented from acting as a director. You will also find it difficult to obtain clients following such a prosecution, as they may be wary of incurring liability themselves should you return to your old ways.

Despite these words of warning, it is important to keep data protection in perspective and understand that most private investigators and debt tracers operate fairly and lawfully.

However, in this field those trying to comply with data protection law can often tread a fine line when it comes to compliance. Here are some other pitfalls to be wary of.

Making an unauthorized disclosure

This is a particularly tricky area for debt tracers, who often put pressure on debtors by letting their families and employers know about the debt. This must be avoided as it amounts to making an unauthorized disclosure in breach of the security principle of the Data Protection Act. It could also give rise to claims for compensation if the individual were to suffer damage as a result of the breach, for example losing their home.

Even if you do not intend to disclose information, the following steps will help you to avoid making accidental disclosures:

- never leave messages about the debt on an answering machine, or make reference to the fact you are a debt collecting agency or debt collector;

- never contact an individual using a work email address or fax;

- if you do contact the individual by telephone or in person make sure that you are talking to the debtor before revealing any information about the debt. Beware of talking to family members with the same name.

CASE STUDY

A debt collection company was investigated by the Information Commissioner after sending faxes to a debtor at her place of work. The faxes contained information about alleged debts and the possible actions that would be taken. The Commissioner found that this was potentially an unauthorized disclosure of the information, and the debt-collecting agency was forced to stop the activity.

Conducting surveillance

If you have been employed to collect information about an individual in a covert manner without their knowledge, make sure that you can justify it under the law. Be particularly careful when collecting sensitive information, such as information about sexual life or health.

Ensuring that your information is correct

If you collect information about an individual from third parties make sure that they are reliable. If you suspect the information may not be accurate do not record it or make any use of it.

Health professionals

Fair and lawful

Health records are defined as sensitive under the Data Protection Act. Any processing by a medical professional will require tighter controls and a regard for both the law and professional conduct. If you breach any duty of confidentiality or other rules governing your profession while processing personal information, you will also be in danger of breaching the Data Protection Act as the processing may be unfair or unlawful.

Allowing access to medical records

Regulations under the Data Protection Act 1998 mean that you can charge more than the statutory fee of £10 for access to paper-based health records, i.e. up to £50, on the basis that this reflects the considerable cost and resources that copying such records entails.

Individuals had access rights under the Access to Health Records Act 1990 until the Data Protection Act 1998 came into force at the beginning of 2000. Requests for health records of deceased individuals are still made under the Access to Health Records Act as the Data Protection Act 1998 applies only to living individuals.

Who can apply?

The following can apply for health information under the Data Protection Act 1998:

- the individual to whom the health information relates;

- a person with parental responsibility where the child is under 18 (16 in Scotland). Parental responsibility arises where the parents have been married, even if they have subsequently divorced, or where the courts have made an order, or where the person has been appointed as a guardian;

- a person acting with power of attorney where individuals are incapable of managing their own affairs;

- a third party instructed by a competent patient, for example a solicitor or insurer. Ensure that you have been provided with a copy of the individual's written consent that pertains to their medical records. If you have any doubts, refer directly to the individual for confirmation.

What information can be released?

Most information can be released to an individual who is making a request to access their own personal information. However, as a health professional, you owe a duty of care to your patient, and if you are being asked to disclose any health information you must first consider whether or not you are the appropriate health professional to make the decision about the disclosure.

Sometimes health information, such as a diagnosis of a terminal illness, might have been withheld from an individual on medical grounds, for example where there was a risk of severe depression or self-harm as a result.

The appropriate health professional who should make the decision about the disclosure will usually be the health professional who has had primary or most recent contact with the individual whose information is to be released, for example the patient's GP or consultant. If you are not this person, you must refer any request for disclosure to them and ask for their permission to disclose. Where there is more than one appropriate health professional, decisions should be taken jointly.

This requirement does not apply where the health information has been provided to you directly by the individual who already has knowledge of the information.

If the request is being made by another party on behalf of the individual concerned, you may withhold information if it is so sensitive that the individual would never have expected it to be released to a third party.

For instance, you may decide not to release information about past venereal diseases, pregnancy terminations or adoptions to third parties, especially close relations.

Confidentiality and security

As a health professional you already understand the importance of protecting patient security. Because you process sensitive personal information you must ensure that the security measures are particularly stringent. If you fail to protect your patients' information you will also find yourself in breach of the Data Protection Act 1998.

Schools

In addition to the areas covered elsewhere in this book, this section looks at those issues that pose particular challenges for schools.

These are likely to include:

- rights of minors and of parents in relation to personal information held;
- education of pupils in relation to data protection.

Rights of minors

The Data Protection Act does not make special provisions for minors. It is the view of the Information Commissioner that if minors have sufficient understanding of their rights under the Data Protection Act, it is they, rather than their parents or guardians, who can exercise these rights.

In England, Wales and Northern Ireland it is accepted that a child over 12 can be expected to have this understanding. The Data Protection Act makes special provisions that bring Scotland in line with these guidelines, as in Scotland a child is not normally expected to have legal capacity until the age of 16.

If a child is not deemed to have this capacity, a parent or guardian can apply on their behalf.

There are special provisions in relation to records held by the state education system, for example that responses to subject access requests are made within 15 school days. There is also a different fee structure that applies to requests for school records, which ranges from £1 for up to 19 pages to a maximum of £50 for any more than 500 pages.

Under the Education (Pupil Information) (England) Regulations 2005, parents have their own right of access to educational files. A fee that covers the cost of providing the information may be set by the governing body.

Data protection education

The Information Commissioner sees understanding of rights under the Data Protection Act as part of the National Curriculum 'Citizenship' programme and has produced a DVD called *Protecting the Plumstones* for secondary level pupils, which can be obtained from the Information Commissioner's website. Special webpages have also been designed to give information about issues commonly affecting children.

Charities, churches and unincorporated not-for-profit organizations

Charities, churches and other not-for-profit organizations are not exempt from the provisions of data protection law just because their functions are carried out 'in a good cause'. The fact that such organizations are primarily involved in assisting others can give rise to complications when it comes to complying with data protection law.

Given the nature of such organizations, you will often find it necessary to process sensitive personal information on individuals with whom you have a relationship, as this sensitive data is implicit in the existence of the relationship, for example members of the church's congregation or a supporter of your organization, which may have religious, political or medical research aims.

Thankfully, there is a specific provision under the Data Protection Act to legitimize the processing of sensitive information in the context of running your organization, as long as you can meet all four of the following conditions.

1. The processing is carried out in the course of the legitimate activities of any body or association that exists for political, philosophical, religious or trade union purposes, and is not established or conducted for profit.

2. The processing is carried out with appropriate safeguards for the rights and freedoms of the individuals.

3. The processing relates to individuals who are members of the body or organization or who have regular contact with it in connection with its purposes.

4. The processing does not involve the disclosure of personal information to a third party without the consent of the individual.

If you cannot meet all four aspects of this basis for processing information, you will have to look at the other grounds for legitimizing the processing of personal information, such as explicit consent.

Publishing information

In order to promote the objectives of your organization, you may use media such as the local press or have a website. It is good practice to ensure you have the agreement of those individuals involved, especially given the wide dissemination of such information. If there is sensitive information involved, it is necessary to obtain consent.

(See Chapter 11, *E-commerce*, for further information.)

Marketing, fundraising and promotion of your organization's goals

Because of the wide definition of marketing under the law, you must ensure that when you carry out your fundraising and promotional activities you respect the right of any individual who objects to you using their information for such purposes. Such activities can be viewed as marketing under the provisions of the law.

Chapter 15 – Maintaining compliance

Now that you understand the obligations the law places upon you and your organization when processing personal information, you should be able to put into practice what you have learnt and stay on the right side of the law with benefits for your organization, customers, clients and employees.

Accountability and responsibility

Unless you are a very small organization you should seek to identify someone to take day-to-day responsibility for the organization's compliance with the Data Protection Act. This will help to ensure that all your practices and procedures remain compliant.

If you have adopted the British Standard on data protection, this will mean appointing a part-time or full-time data privacy officer to be responsible for data protection compliance.

If you have a large business you may want to appoint a separate senior manager or board level officer to be accountable for compliance with the Data Protection Act. This person can delegate day-to-day responsibilities to the data privacy officer but will be accountable should the organization not meet its obligations under the law or the standard. Allocating accountability to a senior level of staff helps ensure that data protection is taken seriously in your organization.

Policies and procedures

If you adopt the standard, you will also need to set up a formal personal information management system (PIMS), i.e. a set of procedures that can help you to comply. A key part of this system involves the development and documentation of a data protection policy that sets out how your organization will process personal information in line with the requirements of the law and the British Standard. If you do adopt such a policy you should ensure that it is visibly supported by your senior management.

The standard includes full details of what such a policy should cover as well as the key requirements of a PIMS. However, even if you do not adopt the standard it will still be a good idea to document your commitment to data protection in a formal policy that makes clear who is responsible and accountable for its implementation.

Regular audit and review

It is important that you carry out regular reviews of the way in which you process personal information. If you are a large organization that is seeking to comply with the British Standard on data protection you will also need to carry out more detailed audits.

Regardless of whether or not you comply with the standard it is still recommended that you review your practices once a year to prepare for re-submitting your annual notification to the Information Commissioner.

Checklists

This book is intended to be used as a reference guide that you can refer to at any time. But as a quick reminder, here are some questions you can ask yourself to make sure you address the most important issues when complying with the law. You can use these checklists as the basis of your annual or other regular reviews of compliance.

Checklist for notification

The following is a checklist for notification.

- Do you know whether or not you are exempt from the requirement to notify the Information Commissioner?

- If you are required to notify, have you done so?

- Is your notification up to date, and does it accurately reflect what you do with personal information?

- Do you know your notification reference number and the date of your next renewal?

Checklist for collecting personal information

The following is a checklist for collecting personal information.

- Can you show that you have a reason for processing the personal information that matches one of the permissible reasons set out by the law?

- Are you processing sensitive personal information? If so, can you show that you meet a ground for processing that matches one of the available grounds set out in the law? Do you need to obtain consent?

- Have you drafted a suitable privacy notice that describes who you are and how the information will be used?

- Are you sure that the way in which you are intending to collect or obtain the information is lawful?

Checklist for using personal information

The following is a checklist for using personal information.

- Does the way in which you use personal information match what you have explained to individuals in any privacy notice or any notification to the Information Commissioner?

- Have you taken measures to ensure the quality of the personal information you process?

- Do you destroy out-of-date information that you no longer require?

- Do you have controls in place to ensure that any storage, disclosure or transfer of personal information is lawful?

- Do you safeguard personal information that is sent outside the EEA?

- Do you take steps to avoid marketing to individuals who have objected to their information being used in this way?

- Are you satisfied that you are aware of any additional data protection requirements that apply to your type of organization?

Checklist for keeping personal information secure

The following is a checklist for keeping personal information secure.

- Have you taken technical measures to secure your personal information?

- Have you trained all your employees in data protection compliance?

- Have you taken steps to protect personal information against fraud?

- Have you put contracts in place with all your data processors?

- Have you made provision for confidential waste disposal where waste may contain personal data?

If you are not sure about your answer for any of these questions, refer back to the relevant section of this book.

However, if you can answer all of these questions positively, you are well on the way to becoming a compliant organization.

Chapter 16 – Contact with the Information Commissioner

Dealing with problems

You have procedures in place, your staff members are trained and it is business as usual, until you receive that call or letter concerning your organization's personal information which puts you on the spot.

This section looks at responding to contact from the Information Commissioner, co-operating with warrants and criminal investigations and handling informal complaints. It also considers the future powers of the Information Commissioner.

Contact from the Information Commissioner

The Information Commissioner is responsible for enforcing the Data Protection Act 1998. There are a number of powers that the Commissioner may exercise in order to fulfil his or her obligation to enforce the law. These include powers to:

- assess whether or not there has been a breach of the law;
- serve an information notice;
- serve an enforcement notice.

The Information Commissioner could make contact with you via a number of different mechanisms depending on what sort of breach of the law may have occurred. Always co-operate with the Information Commissioner's investigations unless you think you may have committed a criminal offence, in which case it is advisable to seek legal advice first.

I've received a letter from the Information Commissioner – What do I do?

There are a number of reasons why you may receive a letter from the Information Commissioner, bearing in mind his or her obligations to encourage good practice as well as to enforce compliance with the Data Protection Act.

Contact from the Information Commissioner could take several forms but if you are being contacted in relation to an alleged breach of the law the process is likely to be that which is described below.

Request for assessment

If an individual contacts the Information Commissioner's Office with a complaint about you, its duty is to assess whether or not you have breached the Data Protection Act, hence the term 'request for assessment'.

The Commissioner will at this point make a verified or unverified assessment. It will be verified if it is a clear cut case of breaching the Data Protection Act, for example failure to notify. It will be unverified because the Commissioner has not yet heard your side of the story.

The letter will ask you for information on a number of points, and ask you to respond within a certain time-frame, usually 28 calendar days.

Handling assessments/requests for assessment

When the Commissioner is satisfied that he or she has all the facts, an assessment will be made as to whether or not you are likely to have complied with the Data Protection Act and what steps will now be taken.

It may be decided that, although you have breached the Data Protection Act, the Commissioner will not take any further action at this time. This is likely to be based on the severity of the breach, and the number of individuals affected, and also the steps you have subsequently put in place to prevent such a breach recurring. This will stay on file, and will be considered should any further complaints be made, especially if they are of a similar nature.

If you receive a letter related to a request for assessment you will need to respond to it promptly, honestly and co-operatively. If you co-operate with the Information Commissioner during this process and follow any advice or recommended actions that are made, the Commissioner is unlikely to take the matter much further unless the circumstances are exceptional.

Formal undertaking

Sometimes an investigation may result in the Information Commissioner requiring a formal undertaking to be signed by the organization committing it to comply with the principles of the Data Protection Act. Failure to meet the conditions of the undertaking is likely to lead to further enforcement action by the Information Commissioner's Office and could result in prosecution.

Information notice

Depending on the severity of the alleged breach of the Data Protection Act, and/ or your co-operation with a request for assessment, the Commissioner may choose to serve an 'information notice'. This is a request for you to provide information relating to your compliance with the principles within a certain time-frame. If you do not supply the information you will be committing a criminal offence.

An information notice is rarely served but may be more likely where you have failed to co-operate or are refusing to supply information.

The Commissioner has had, to date, few occasions to use this power. This implies that organizations choose to co-operate with investigations.

Enforcement notice

If the Commissioner believes that you are breaching the data protection principles, he or she can serve an 'enforcement notice', which requires the organization to process or to stop processing information in a certain way. Compliance with the notice will ensure compliance with the data protection principles.

If you receive an enforcement notice, it is advisable to seek legal advice. You have two options:

1. to comply with the notice within the specified time-frame, or

2. to appeal against the notice to the Information Tribunal.

Can I appeal against information and enforcement notices?

If you disagree with the serving of or the contents of the notice, you can appeal within the time-frames given in the notice to the Information Tribunal. This is an independent body consisting of representatives from both commercial and individuals' groups.

They will:

• agree with the notice; or

• disagree with the notice; or

• suggest revised wording for the notice (this last option is the most common approach taken).

If you have received a notice from the Commissioner, it is advisable to seek legal advice. If you are a small organization you may want to co-operate with any enforcement notice rather than facing the expense of an appeal to the Tribunal. If you are considering an appeal you should know that the Information

Commissioner rarely loses. The regulator is usually fairly sure of the grounds on which an enforcement notice is issued.

What is the difference between enforcement and prosecution?

Under the Data Protection Act there are a number of criminal offences. The individual or organization concerned, as with other criminal offences under any other law, is prosecuted by the courts, not by the Information Commissioner.

A breach of the principles is not a criminal offence, although the Commissioner has powers to 'enforce' compliance. Noncompliance with the enforcement measures could, however, mean you see your day in court.

By reading this book you have taken proactive steps to understand the requirements of the Data Protection Act and what these mean for your organization, and ultimately to prevent either criminal or civil action against you or your organization. However, it is important to understand the extent of the repercussions should there be an issue.

The criminal offences covered in this book are:

- failure to notify;

- failure to keep a notification up to date;

- failure to comply with a request for the notification information where you are exempt;

- failure to comply with an information/enforcement notice;

- knowingly or recklessly giving a false statement in relation to an information notice;

- knowingly or recklessly giving a false statement in relation to an enforcement notice;

- obtaining, disclosing or seeking the disclosure of information without the consent of the organization concerned.

Who is liable?

Any sole trader, partner or company and where applicable, its directors, senior managers and secretaries are liable where they have consented to, or failed to prevent, a breach of the Data Protection Act.

Individuals can also commit offences under the Data Protection Act, where they knowingly or recklessly use information without the consent of the organization responsible for the personal information.

For further information see Chapter 13, *Security and disposal of personal information.*

Warrant to search premises

If the Commissioner has reasonable grounds to suspect that you have or are committing a criminal offence under the Data Protection Act or are breaching any of the data protection principles, he or she can apply to a judge for a warrant to enter and search the premises where it is believed there will be evidence. Obstructing the execution of a warrant is a criminal offence.

The Commissioner will generally apply for a warrant where previous requests for assistance from you have not been met. You can avoid the official knock on the door by being co-operative.

What happens if I am prosecuted?

You should always take the advice of a criminal lawyer if you are being prosecuted under the law. They will advise you on how to plead.

Criminal proceedings (with the exception of obstructing a search warrant) are heard in either the Magistrates' Court or Crown Court (Sheriff Court or High Court of Justiciary in Scotland). If found guilty, the fines are up to £5,000 in the Magistrates' Court, and are not capped in the Crown Court.

Dealing with informal complaints from individuals

If you want to avoid drawing yourself to the attention of the Information Commissioner and being dragged through a formal investigation process your best bet is to deal with informal complaints from individuals efficiently and quickly before they escalate.

Here are a few tips.

- Always treat a complaint about the way personal information is being used seriously.

- Respond quickly to the complaint and investigate the individual's concern.

- If you believe the complaint is justified act quickly to put things right and consider compensating the individual.

- Keep a record of how and when any complaint was resolved.

- If the complaint showed up a weakness in your existing systems put this right to avoid further complaints being made.

Changes to the Information Commissioner's powers

In 2008, it was announced that the Information Commissioner is to be given stronger powers to regulate the Data Protection Act under the Criminal Justice and Immigration Act 2008. These powers will allow the Information Commissioner to serve 'monetary penalty notices' (essentially fines) on organizations that deliberately or negligently commit a serious breach of any of the data protection principles. It is also possible that new prison sentences of up to 12 months could be introduced for serious offences.

Before serving the monetary penalty notice, the Commissioner must give the organization notice of its intent to do so, so that the organization has a chance to make representations. The organization can also appeal to the Information Tribunal if it does not agree with the Information Commissioner's judgement.

Other changes include the power to carry out unannounced checks of government departments and public authorities ensuring that they fully comply with the Data Protection Act; and for any person, served a warrant, to provide evidence that they are complying with the Act and to determine a deadline and location for the information to be given.

Refer to the Information Commissioner's website for further information on these changes, and how they may affect you.

Bibliography

British Standards

BS 7799, *Information security management systems*
BS 10012, *Data Protection — Specification for a personal information management system*
ISO 27001, *Information technology — Security techniques — Information security management*

Table of Statutes

Adults with Incapacity (Scotland) Act 2000, 2000 asp 4, London, OPSI, 2000
Access to Health Records Act 1990, 1990 CHAPTER 23, London, OPSI, 1990
Child Maintenance and Other Payments Act 2008, 2008 CHAPTER 6, London, OPSI, 2008
Computer Misuse Act 1990, 1990 CHAPTER 18, London, OPSI, 1990
Criminal Justice and Immigration Act 2008, 2008 CHAPTER 4, London, OPSI, 2008
Data Protection Act 1998, 1998 CHAPTER 29, London, OPSI, 1998
Financial Services and Markets Act 2000, 2000 CHAPTER 8, London, OPSI, 2000
Mental Capacity Act 2005, 2005 CHAPTER 9, London, OPSI, 2005
Taxes Management Act 1970, 1970 CHAPTER 9, London, OPSI, 1970

Table of Statutory Instruments

Statutory Instrument 2003 No. 3183, The Control of Misleading Advertisements (Amendment) Regulations 2003, London, OPSI, 2003
Statutory Instrument 2004 No. 1039, The Privacy and Electronic Communications (EC Directive) (Amendment) Regulations 2004, London, OPSI, 2004
Statutory Instrument 2005 No. 1437, The Education (Pupil Information) (England) Regulations 2005, London, OPSI, 2005

European Directives

European Union Data Protection Directive 95/46/EC, European Commission, 1995

Information Commissioner's Office Publications

ICO, *Annual Reports*, London, OPSI, 2001–2008

ICO, *CCTV Code of Practice*, London, OPSI, 2008

ICO, *The Lights are on*, London, OPSI, 2007

ICO, *Monitoring at Work*, London, OPSI

ICO, *Privacy Notices Code of Practice*, London, OPSI, 2009

ICO, *Protecting the Plumstones*, London, OPSI

Sources of information

Information Commissioner's Office

The Information Commissioner's Office is the UK regulator through which notification is conducted. It also provides guidance, and written and verbal advice.

UK Head Office

Information Commissioner's Office
Wycliffe House
Water Lane
Wilmslow
SK9 5AF

Telephone:
Enquiries 01625 545745
Notification 01625 545740
Switchboard 01625 545700
Fax: 01625 524510
DX: 20819

Email:
General: mail@ico.gov.uk
Notification: data@notification.demon.co.uk
Website: www.informationcommissioner.gov.uk

Scotland Office

The Information Commissioner's Office – Scotland
93–95 Hanover Street
Edinburgh
EH2 1DJ

Telephone: 0131 301 5071
Email: Scotland@ico.gsi.gov.uk

Wales Office

Information Commissioner's Office – Wales
Cambrian Buildings
Mount Stuart Square
Cardiff
CF10 5FL

Telephone: 029 2044 8044
Fax: 029 2044 8045
Email: wales@ico.gsi.gov.uk

Northern Ireland Office

The Information Commissioner's Office – Northern Ireland
51 Adelaide Street
Belfast
BT2 8FE

Telephone: 028 9026 9380
Fax: 028 9026 9388
Email: ni@ico.gsi.gov.uk

Standards and templates

British Standards Institution

BSI provides training and seminars, including ISEB certificate courses on data protection and freedom of information.

BSI also publishes the information security standard BS 7799.

Address:
389 Chiswick High Road
London
W4 4AL

Telephone: 020 8996 9000
Fax: 020 8996 7001
Email: cservices@bsigroup.com
Website: www.bsigroup.com